"Having engaged in political campaigns and elections for nearly 50 years, I consider Life in the Fishbowl mandatory reading for everyone contemplating a run for elected office. Full of insightful advice, frank discussion and respect for public service, this little book should be read before, during, and after the campaign—win or lose. The authors keep it real with many personal lessons, keen observations, and helpful recommendations."

The Honorable Mickey Ibarra, Assistant to the President, The White House (1997-2001)

"...if I were still teaching my course on political campaigns, I'd make *Life in the FishBowl* assigned reading (I wish I could do that for prospective candidates)."

Terry Christensen, Emeritus Professor of Political Science, San Jose State University

"I wish Life in the Fishbowl had been available when I first ran for office. It's a practical guide filled with apt insights into what's it really like to run for office. And running for partisan office, like I did, can be especially ugly. The toll on your family and marriage can't be an afterthought when you step into the public arena. My favorite chapter is "Pitfalls of Public Service" where they share how to differentiate between friends and merely allies and drive home those moments of truth when you have to say no to a friend or supporter. In short, Guisselle and Ron have written a superb book to help prepare and guide candidates and their families to face the pressures of public life— both the joy and grief that comes right after announcing your candidacy."

Jim Cunneen, former California State Assemblymember

"Being a parent today already puts you under a microscope. Being elected puts that microscope on display for everyone. As a working mother who also started and raised a family while growing a political career, I wish I had this book a decade ago! This is a unique book. It's practical, not philosophical. This is the type of book I could see myself gifting a candidate in the future. Thanks Guisselle and Ron for taking the time to pass your knowledge on to the next generation of leaders."

Giselle Hale, former Mayor of Redwood City, Technology Executive and Mom of two, young girls

"One of a kind and a must-read book! As a former political candidate, campaign manager, and staff to elected officials, I know first-hand the struggles that candidates, elected officials and their families face with work, public scrutiny, stress, and life balance. This book will honestly guide anyone who is either asked to run or even considering running for any public office. It shares the secrets of the political world that are known but never spoken about."

Edesa Bitbadal, Founder/CEO,
Elevate Now Consulting, LLC,
former political candidate
and staff

Life in the
Fishbowl

Lessons *to* Help *you* Survive *and* Thrive *in* Elected Office

---

Guisselle Nuñez and Ron Gonzales

Foreword by Terry Christensen

Paperback ISBN: 9798874256210
IngramSparks ISBN: 9798869198464

Published through Rising Above Publishing Services

www.risingabovepublishingservices.com

Edited by David Vossbrink

PREFACE

"I am interested in telling my particular truth as I have seen it." -Gwendolyn Brooks.

This book has taken approximately four years to write. We were on a roll for about one year with monthly interviews of current and former elected officials and their spouses until life hit us in the form of the COVID-19 pandemic and our own divorce. But we are back, as friends, to finish this book and share the lessons of our experience.

As you read this book, the thought may cross your mind of how we can give advice on this topic, including the spouse and family role, if we are now divorced. You should know we were together for twenty years and married for sixteen years. Twelve of those married years took place after Ron ended his elected role, and we're proud of the partnership we had throughout.

Ron had both positive and negative experiences when he served in elected office, and our strong partnership helped us through them all. But often in life, as you focus on one thing, you may lose focus on other important matters. Our time together as a couple may have ended, but the life lessons, our love, and our work together to support our community remain. Thus, we have come back together to finish this project and share those experiences and insights with you.

The idea for this book started through Guisselle's personal branding work through the years, as spouses of local elected officials would come to her for advice and an empathetic ear on how to deal with life in the political fishbowl.

Being married to someone who holds public office can be a lonely experience, especially if you're brand new to it. There's no welcoming party for the spouse (or even the candidate after election night), nor a handbook to tell you how to manage the craziness, the accolades, and the stress, or to teach you how to differentiate among allies, friends, and foes.

Much of it is on-the-job training, learning from your errors, and attempting to look graceful when you've stumbled. And, yes, you can expect every stumble to be magnified and interpreted in the least generous manner.

Here is a quick backstory for additional context...

Having worked on political campaigns and for Ron when he served as Mayor for the City of San Jose, Guisselle had some idea of what married life

to an elected official would be like– the crazy schedule, the politics, the instant "fast" friends who come
into your life, the fear of saying something to someone, however innocently, that will be interpreted the
worst way possible.

Our story started under the blinding glare of
the media's intense spotlight and relentless narra-
tive machine that relishes in creating caricatures of
villains and heroes, irrespective of the truth. We
made the "mistake" of falling in love while working together in City Hall. Ron had recently sepa-
rated from his wife and was twenty-three years older
than Guisselle. We say "mistake" tongue in cheek
because we considered our relationship mostly a
private matter. But recalling the vitriol surrounding
events at the time, it was surprising just how many
people considered our relationship relevant to the
state of the city and thereby unforgivable.

We'll let the reader imagine how irresistible
this story was for a media more interested in the
frenzied gossip that flows through City Hall than
the nuts and bolts of running a city for a million
people. A perfect example of your life in a fishbowl:
no place to hide.

Guisselle's introduction to the role of a political
spouse was jarring. She would have very much appreciated some friendly advice from another spouse

willing to offer support, their lessons learned, or advice from their experiences in political life.

In retrospect, perhaps this was not realistic, and she had to learn it on the fly. That's the reason why she has always been ready to share lessons from her own journey with other spouses who seek her out. And, in many ways, that is the catalyst for this book.

Ron's twenty-four years of public service as a Sunnyvale Council member and Mayor, Santa Clara County Supervisor and Board Chair, and Mayor of San Jose causes many candidates to seek his advice about running for election. Ron's first question is always: "Why are you running for office?" Much of the time, he finds the candidates do not have a clear idea of their "why" or any idea of the challenges that await them.

So, we blended our two experiences into this idea of writing a "what to expect when you're expecting" but aimed at those folks (and their families) considering running for public office.

This is more of a story of "what is" rather than "what should be." The reality is that fear, uncertainty, and mistrust are clouds that constantly hang over you while serving in office. You are reluctant to share authentic moments or to offer your true personal feelings (even to those you think are "political friends or allies") because it may show "weakness" and be used against you or your spouse at some point.

We interviewed over a dozen former and current elected officials and their spouses, and at the heart of our discussion was the essential question, "What do you know now that you wish you had known before or while you were running?"

In the following pages, we share their answers to this question, among many other stories. We send a heartfelt thank you and gratitude to everyone who chose to be vulnerable with us by sharing their stories and their own paths to elected office—win or lose.

Due to a number of practical constraints, we focused our interviews on elected officials we knew and were local to the San Francisco Bay Area. Individual stories and journeys may differ, but we are confident that the themes and lessons we heard resonate across geographical or political lines and speak to a common experience of serving and living in elected public service.

Some elected officials and their spouses we invited to participate did, however, decline to be interviewed because they weren't comfortable sharing their personal stories. That's actually why we wrote this book because we know that being vulnerable in this business is difficult and risky. We extend our understanding to those who declined our offer to participate this time.

Ultimately, we want this book to serve as a guide to a side of politics no one talks about. A guide that provides candidates and their families with knowledge, awareness, and inspiration so they may be successful, make good choices, and thrive in the fishbowl.

Running for public office and serving can be exhilarating, infuriating, and intimidating all at the same time. None of it is easy, and you may not see the full rewards until years after your service. We wanted to be authentic about the challenges ahead for you and your family. But we also want to help you find comfort in finding that others have felt the same way as you and yet found ways to work through those challenges to thrive and succeed. You are not alone.

We thank all of those who allowed us into their lives and were willing to be vulnerable and courageous with us—and share their stories so that their journey may inspire you and your families on your journey in this noble profession of public service.

"Being a politician is a poor profession. Being a public servant is a noble one."-Herbert Hoover, 31st U.S. President

Guisselle and Ron

FOREWORD

Are you ready for this?

Most people soliciting advice about running for office answer this question by discussing fundraising, endorsements, volunteers, and maybe campaign strategy.

These will come up later in the conversation but what I'm trying to get at with that question is whether they're personally ready for what it will take to run and to serve, should they be elected. How will they cope with criticisms and defeats? Or the hit piece an opponent will surely do dredging up some minor (or major) social or legal misstep or misstatement long in the past? Or the betrayal of someone they thought was a friend and supporter?

These questions apply not only to the prospective candidates but also to their families and loved ones. Are they ready? How will they cope with such criticisms, attacks, and betrayals? It's not unusual these days for the spouses and even the children of candidates or officeholders to get caught up in the vitriol of politics.

For candidates who may not actually be ready for what lies ahead for them and even for those who think they are ready, *Life in the Fishbowl* should be required reading – and maybe for their spouses and close friends as well.

Guisselle Nuñez and Ron Gonzales have been there—Ron as a candidate and officeholder at several levels of local government and Guisselle as a staffer, consultant, and spouse of an officeholder. They went through trying times—crucifixion by the media, abandonment by allies, and even social shunning—with aplomb and dignity. It would be understandable if after all this they chose to walk away from politics and public service and never look back. Instead—to their great credit—they've each in their way continued to serve their community.

Additionally, they've written *Life in the Fishbowl* to prepare future candidates and officeholders for what to expect and how to cope. If you've never been up close and personal with a political campaign, some of what they write about may seem unlikely or inconsequential but none of it is. They interviewed many other candidates and officeholders for their book, and they all have stories to tell about challenges they and their spouses faced and often were unprepared for. I guess that these other officeholders appreciated the opportunity to reflect on their experiences. Come to think of it, current officeholders—not just candidates—could also benefit from a quick read of *Life in the Fishbowl*.

What's more, if I were still teaching my course on political campaigns, I'd make *Life in the Fishbowl* assigned reading (I wish I could do that for prospective candidates). The typical text on campaigns focuses on the mechanics: structuring a campaign staff and organization, fundraising, mobilizing, and managing volunteers, opposition research, collecting endorsements, media relations, campaign media, tactics, and strategy, etc. All are crucial to a successful campaign. But none of these get to the personal experiences of the candidates or their families or staff and they need to know and understand that personal stress and emotions will also be part of their experience. *Life in the Fishbowl* is a great reminder of this and excellent preparation for candidates, families, staff, and key supporters.

In case you think *Life in the Fishbowl* is making mountains out of molehills, think again. If life in politics could be rough when Ron was in office—nearly two decades ago—it's exponentially tougher now. The polarization and vitriol of national politics is readily apparent but alarmingly, it's seeped down to local politics, too—it's just less apparent because of the decline of media coverage at the local level. Yet, it's there, and every now and then it breaks out in places where local politics is traditionally polite and mostly a bit boring. Angry speakers take over meetings of school boards and city councils large and small. Zoom meetings are crashed by hate-spewing speakers who may not even be residents of the community. Demonstrators show up at officeholders' homes; families are threatened.

All this is why *Life in the Fishbowl* is essential reading for candidates, officeholders, and their families.

So… Are you ready for this?

Terry Christensen
Emeritus Professor of Political Science
San Jose State University

Terry is a longtime observer and active participant in local politics in San Jose and the South Bay. As a professor, he taught courses on local government, interest groups and political campaigns. He's authored or co-authored books on local government, California politics and political movies and was host of CreaTV's Valley Politics for eight years, interviewing dozens of candidates and current and past officeholders (including Ron Gonzales).

This book is dedicated to our family
and friends who stood by us through all the highs
and lows we experienced while Ron served in
elected office.
And we also dedicate this book to all who are
considering and those already serving in public
office. May your journey to serve be filled with
joy, success, and discovery.

TABLE OF CONTENTS

xvii

INTRODUCTION

"...elected office and highly visible public office, takes a toll, and you have to be prepared for it..." - Jim Hartnett, former Redwood City, CA Councilmember and Mayor

In life, what is unsaid is often what we most need to know. This may be especially true when running for elected office. Entering the political arena can often feel like you're blindly navigating a maze in front of highly vocal and opinionated spectators. It's living life inside a fishbowl, and it can be a lonely place. There's no instruction manual. There's no welcoming committee. It is rare when anyone opens up to you and is willing to share with you their experiences and those hard-learned lessons.

But why is it that those in elected office (and their spouses) don't share those lessons with newcomers? After all, for better or for worse, anyone who wins elected office is a member of a small club. You'd be forgiven for thinking that would give rise to a certain camaraderie. But the reality is that trust is a rare commodity in politics and genuine friendships are scarce.

This may appear to state the obvious, but at the risk of sounding naive, when you're new and bright-eyed and bushy tailed, the thickness and deepness of the muck is surprising. Surprisingly, it can be harder to trust when you're serving on the same dais. Even though you should expect a commonality of interest serving the same community, there is always a fear that sharing your personal thoughts and vulnerabilities will be used against you in a future campaign, the next mailer, the next social media post, the next vote, or end up as the subject of voyeuristic gossip. That's politics. Not as it should be—but as it often is.

There are plenty of books and articles on how to manage a winning political campaign and plenty of political campaign consultants whose job is to help you do just that. This is not that type of book.

This one's for you, the aspiring candidate, the freshly elected official, and your families. This is the stuff that no one talks about until it's too late when you are frustrated, sad, angry, and disillusioned. You may still feel that way along your public service journey, but perhaps some knowledge that others have been there too and that you are not alone can bring solace and hope to continue the road ahead.

We believe that if you are going to jump into the swimming pool, you should at least know how deep the pool is and how to tread water. Our goal is not to talk or recruit anybody into running for elected office. Our goal is to provide you with information in the form of lessons that will provide you with some of the knowledge, advice, and inspiration that you'll need to swim in that pool, that political fishbowl.

We share fifteen of the most important lessons we've learned from our own experience and from our conversations with other elected officials and their spouses.

Here's a summary of those lessons:

Chapter 1: Taking the Leap

Lesson 1: You and your partner need to understand that running for elected office and thereafter serving in public office will never follow a normal 8-5 schedule.

Lesson 2: Do opposition research on yourself.

Lesson 3: Don't decide to run for office without speaking to your spouse and family first.

Lesson 4: Be clear about the role your spouse wants to play in your public life.

Chapter 2: What's your "Why?"

Lesson 5: If you are being courted to run, never assume that these same leaders will be with you during the campaign.

The road during your public service will have many potholes (excuse the city government pun). But it will also have many moments along the way where you will feel exhilarated and fulfilled for what you have helped your community achieve to make it better.

It is never too early to prepare for such a responsibility, and it is never too late to learn from experienced role models. One of the most important lessons shared by all interviewees, and something they wish they would have done before taking the leap, was to take the time to prepare to make their decision to run for office. By reading this book, you and your families can begin the journey of exploration, reflection, and knowledge.

CHAPTER 1

Taking The Leap

On May 9, 1940, the day Winston Churchill became Prime Minister, his wife Clementine Churchill was asked by their children to give a toast on the occasion. She then followed by sharing this story.

> *"Some of you may not know that on the eve of our marriage I got cold feet…but the real reason for my wintery feet was that I knew, even then, that his priority would be public life and it worried a young girl greatly, this wretched thought of eternally coming second. But so it has proven to be, and in due course our children would have to make peace with that same fact. We all did, you see, in our own way. And now today, we are to receive our reward, proof that our small sacrifice was for a far, far, greater good"* (Imperial War Museums, 2018).

Political life   ou and the   shbowl

Elected office and a life in politics are not unlike other industries: you need to learn to maneuver through an organization, its political system, and its key players so that you can make policy and carry it out. A critical difference between these two worlds, however, is that in elected office, your every move is analyzed, second guessed, and criticized, often in a very public manner.

Getting a majority of those votes you need, gaining community support, navigating headlines, and making the related tradeoffs and compromises can lead to wariness or mistrust among both allies and opponents. It's rare that these players will stick their neck out to offer advice to newcomers.

There is a great vulnerability involved in sharing how you feel and think about your elected work, so every elected official must learn these lessons on their own. This is the paradox of public service: what you think would be the most challenging, the campaign, is not; it's what comes next, living your life in the fishbowl for all to see.

Your first order of business, if you are interested in serving in elected office, is to seriously assess why you want to run. Find out what's involved during a campaign, serving in office, balancing an intense schedule, losing your privacy, and how all of this will affect your family, yourself, and your personal life.

Most candidates can give a ten-point summary of what they want to do once in office, but they generally won't have a clear idea of truly why they are running for office. Saying, "It's my time," or "I want to fix this or that, or "I have the right skills and experience" is not enough. You must know your "why"; what or who inspired you, what are your stories that formed your decision, why you now?

Knowing "what's your why?" along with a realistic awareness of the challenges that come from living in the fishbowl are essential to achieving your goals while maintaining balance with other areas of your life. What you will face and how you will manage issues and people will affect your relationship with yourself, your family, and your career in and out of the office. It's best to be prepared.

> *Until you value yourself, you will not value your time. Until you value your time, you will not do anything with it. -M. Scott Peck*

Lesson 1. You and your partner need to understand that running for elected office, and then serving in public office, will never be a normal 8-5 job.

Life in public service, especially for elected officials, doesn't hold normal office hours. It begins just like that too—many enter a campaign while also working a full- time job. It's hard to fathom the amount of time it will take to manage your regular day job, your family obligations, and time for self-care while also making time to conduct relentless campaign tasks such as precinct walking, community meetings, and fundraising— itself a full-time job.

In a study conducted in 2018 by members of the British Parliament, Ashley Weinberg found that 92% of the members worked in excess of 50-70 hours per week (Flinders et al., 2018). That doesn't include the burden and sleepless nights from emotional stressors caused by conflicting public expectations, underlain by public mistrust, and the intense competition you have from colleagues and voters. And all of this is playing out on the very public stage. We were unable to find any similar studies conducted in the United States, but anecdotally, we can find many similarities of this study to that of elected life in the United States.

As Guisselle continues to provide support to spouses who seek her counsel, whether they are in campaign mode or their spouses are serving in elected office, the number one issue that they constantly struggle with is related to the "schedule." They now must either juggle full-time jobs with a campaign or a full-time job with a "part-time" elected office role.

Once in office, the schedule now includes a full-time elected official role and an exorbitant demand to attend and prepare for community meetings, public and political events, council meetings, and much more, usually evenings and weekends. The schedule needs to fit all of the above, plus try to integrate a normal family, personal, and professional life.

We say "integrate" because we know from experience that true "work-life balance" will be hard to attain. You will need to learn how to build boundaries and priorities around your scheduling demands so that you can integrate your family, personal, and professional lives with your public service demands.

It won't be easy. It will take commitment, discipline, and some time to try things out and modify them as you see what works and what doesn't work for you. But the candidate/elected official and their spouse must be super clear about their respective priorities, what is non-negotiable, and what they each need from each other to provide vital support.

For those on the campaign trail, you may need to use your home (AKA your garage) as your campaign headquarters, at least until you raise enough money to move into an office. Until then, you may have volunteers visiting your home at odd hours to help stuff envelopes, walk precincts, collect signs and flyers, etc. You may feel like you need to feed folks to thank them for their support, and candidates have been known to share the breakfast that the spouse was cooking for their kids.

Sometimes, the spouse's reaction isn't the most positive one at that moment, but this is all doable if your family is onboard and you have help. Nevertheless, be aware that all of this can be taxing on you and the whole family.

Let's face it: it can even be taxing on your neighbors. Letitia Clark, Councilmember and former Mayor for the City of Tustin, CA, remembers when her family moved into a new neighborhood. She made a concerted effort to make sure her neighbors knew that she served in public office, and therefore, they may see a lot of activity around her house. This included local news vans parked in front of her home or staff members coming to her house to pick up items (which would still lead to neighbors calling her to let her know there were strangers walking around her house, etc.). She tried to reach out to her neighbors to help them understand the activities surrounding her role so they didn't feel that having her family as neighbors was a burden. And these days, elected officials (and their neighbors) should also expect occasional public protests in front of their homes.

Once you are in office, you have weeknight and weekend events, preparation for multiple board, council, and committee meetings, and the meetings themselves that perennially run late. Letitia has estimated that between her part-time elected position and her full-time job, she could easily spend 40-60 hours per week on each role.

That will squeeze your family life if you have defined your priorities and your boundaries. Ensure that you and your spouse are in constant communication about expectations related to this new and wacky schedule.

Raul Peralez, former City of San Jose Councilmember, and his wife, Victoria Ramirez, realized the importance of this soon after Raul won his council seat. They both were intentional about having empathy for one another. They said, "We two need to be a team, not enemies, so the point is to understand, compromise, and find a solution."

Victoria stressed "making an effort to be in your partner's shoes, especially when you had no relationship to politics prior to being together." This will allow you both to compromise from a neutral standpoint rather than from a personal and emotional one. They said, "You must be able to grab the reins of the key decisions that affect your relationships, or otherwise they will be made for you."

Even Arnold Schwarzenegger admitted in his Netflix docuseries "Arnold" that his schedule while California governor greatly affected his relationship with his wife and children. So, no one is immune—not even "the Governator" to the pressures and the demands of a political life and its schedule.

Here are questions to reflect on as you integrate your public and private work/life schedules:

- Will your partner be all right with your possibly being gone late at night many days of the week? How does your family schedule compare to where you'll need to be visible in the community or attend mandatory meetings?

- What are some things that are non-negotiable for you and your spouse related to managing your personal, professional, and family schedule?

- How will you ensure you communicate your scheduling priorities to your staff and colleagues? Your staff will always want to book as many events and meetings as possible. But it's up to you to determine the boundaries that work for you and your family life.

As you educate your staff about your boundaries for scheduling, you will also help the community understand your priorities.

Clarity about what is important to you and your partner is key, which leads to the next set of questions you must answer to set up limits that will guide your time during the campaign and when in office.

- What days and/or hours of the week do you both agree to commit to spending undisturbed with your family and each other?

  For example, what does dinner time look like for you and your family? How are you showing up for these undisturbed times with your family? Can everyone put their phones down and practice mindfulness together?

- When will I make time for myself? For example, how will I fit in time for exercise, personal time, mental and emotional health, leisure reading, self-care, time to eat during the day, and adequate sleep?

We may think it's a given that we will make time "to eat during the day," but you will be surprised how often that doesn't happen. Guisselle remembers spouses telling her that their elected spouses would come home at 9 p.m. and not have eaten yet after skipping lunch. We say to you, the elected spouse/candidate, that it is up to you to prioritize and make sure your staff knows that you need time to eat. You have got to be at your optimal mental and emotional health to manage all that is in front of you.

Santa Clara County Supervisor Susan Ellenberg and her husband Steve remember that during the campaign, priorities around diet, exercise, and even down time with friends went out the window. Susan felt guilty about doing anything that wasn't focused on the campaign. And even though they were walking precincts, they both gained weight from not having a proper diet and eating too much fast food. Only after she had been elected did they realize they were still exhibiting some of the bad habits they had picked up during the campaign.

While we are on the topic of eating—one thing Ron and I learned from 20+ years of attending events is to eat before you go! It may sound funny, but you'll find a lot of high-calorie appetizers, alcohol, and junk food served at public events. No one shared this tip with us, and we admit we didn't stick to this rule as well as we should have, especially because no one shared this tip with us. Believe it, there's such a thing as the "freshman 10" pounds for elected officials. (So be aware and plan so you can eat regular, healthy meals as much as possible.

Whether on the campaign trail or when you're in office, also be aware that holidays are not your days off. Incoming City of San Jose Mayor Matt Mahan was quoted in the Silicon Valley Business Journal by Moss (2022) saying that on his first day on the job, New Year's Day, he would spend the day visiting and thanking fire and police officers and other community organizations. Every holiday is an opportunity to visit with your constituents and the community. And though that may be necessary, we still recommend you reflect on what your boundaries for time off look like for you.

Councilmember Raul Peralez and his wife, Victoria Ramirez, were aware they needed to make sacrifices, but they were also adamant that balance would be essential to their lives. California State Assemblymember Ash Kalra reminded us that it will take some time to get your partner or spouse and your family used to the new routines, but your mutual flexibility and reflection will allow you to find ways to keep the quality time you need.

Ron also went into office with a similar time structure that he implemented during his election and public service that prioritized his family and relationships. Sundays became Ron's day off to spend with his family, as it was Raul's. They both were clear about this to their staff. Additionally, Ron also asked his staff to give him two nights off from attending community events during the work week.

The community and your staff–and your own drive–will always want you to do something more. So, you'll get used to squeezing in one, two, or three more community events–and you may think, "I can do it." but it all adds up to your personal time being eaten away. Yes, it's important to be visible and attend events and meetings, but those activities cannot come at the sacrifice of your mental health, your family priorities, and your plain physical need to rest and recuperate.

If you have a team, they might be able to attend some of these events on your behalf. Like any other "regular" job, without boundaries and a distinction between your work and personal time, the result will be hardship for your relationships, and you risk eventually burning out.

> *"Politicians report surprisingly low levels of perceived control over their job compared to the rest of the working population." As mentioned in the Washington Post, August 16, 2021 article, "A politician's mental health is as crucial as a pilot's. Why don't we tend to it?"* (Weinberg, 2021).

We are all human, and we all are granted the same amount of time each day. The community, your staff, and even your family may forget that fact. The pressures we put on ourselves to meet one more group and attend one more event, at the sacrifice of our mental, physical, and emotional health, maybe a noble one, but in the end, it is a disservice to you, your family, and your community.

Preparing for the campaign. Do you have skeletons in your closet?

Lesson 2. Do opposition research on yourself.

Be clear and honest with yourself about past incidents in your life that could be used by your opposition or the news media that could be misconstrued or distorted or that will need complex explanations during your campaign.

Doing opposition research on yourself will help you better prepare your family for negative accusations or comments that might be said about you. It's easy to take offense or become defensive when you're facing criticism, shaming, and false accusations of you or your loved ones.

Be brutally honest with yourself and discuss any potential issues with your campaign consultant. More likely than not, your opponent or an enterprising reporter will find something to say about whatever it is you are not saying.

We're talking about youthful indiscretions, a crazy in-law or disreputable cousin, money or tax troubles, regrettable social media posts, personal health or relationship issues, prior inconvenient political enthusiasms, embarrassing photos from your college reunions, negative performance reviews–the list goes on.

You'll need to have a strategy, a plan, and solid responses at the ready. But you also must include your family in those discussions and revelations. They too, need to know what's hidden in your closet and how to answer any questions about it that may come up in their daily life. A prudent rule for you and your spouse: No surprises.

Even if you have a clean slate and no skeletons in your closet, it's always a good idea to think of anyone or any group who may want to run a smear campaign on you.

For example, a candidate in a recent Bay Area city council election had to confront decades-old domestic abuse allegations raised by an opposing candidate. A local political committee that had originally endorsed this candidate withdrew its endorsement and asked the candidate to end his bid for city council.

The candidate said these allegations from twenty years prior were never true, and they were originally made in the context of a bitter divorce and custody battle. Regardless, the committee's decision to rescind its endorsement was momentous and became a turning point in the campaign.

Nothing is guaranteed to remain private in this business, and this example underscores the need to be proactive with what opponents and critics can say during or after a political campaign, and all too often, truth alone is an insufficient defense.

Another recent example involved a San Jose council appointment. Five remaining applicants hoped to be picked by the city council to fill a vacancy. But *San Jose Spotlight* reported that "three of the five are facing individual allegations of wage theft, domestic abuse or concerns about residency in the district" (Geha, 2023). Were these allegations accurate? Who knows, but the damage is done. As we have mentioned, you need to be honest about your background and history because, inevitably, it will always come out in the open.

Have you talked to your spouse and family?

We live in an era where everything is "fair game" when it comes to the media–all media. Running for elected office means you have even more of a reason to do the necessary work to prepare your family to avoid surprises and problems.

This means communication, especially if it's uncomfortable. First and foremost, discussing with your partner their feelings about you running for office should happen before you make the joint public announcement. That decision will inevitably affect their life just as much as yours. If you do not have the support of your spouse, then we highly suggest rethinking your decision to run for office. So, the next lesson:

Lesson 3. Don't decide to run for office without speaking to your spouse and family first

Steve Guerrero, a community leader, was encouraged by other leaders to campaign for a seat on a school board just a few days before the filing deadline. He decided to go for it, but he made the decision without consulting anyone else. Most importantly, he didn't talk with his wife, Lisa.

When Steve eventually told Lisa, he said he had not talked to her first because of the short time to meet the filing deadline.

He realized then this was his first campaign mistake. Steve shared in his interview with us that his decision also came from listening to his ego. It was flattering when other community leaders approached him to say he was capable and could do the job. He felt honored, and it felt good.

But as the old saying goes, "You don't know what you don't know." He had no idea what he was signing up for, and he thought to himself, "Wow, I'm really getting the red-carpet treatment. How could I lose?" So, he said yes. Soon enough, he found out those same folks who asked him to run weren't there for him during the campaign.

That night, after he had said yes to running, Steve came home and told his wife. Lisa wasn't at all happy. She shared that she had wished "Steve knew what he was getting into before he made the decision without me. I was disappointed because he really didn't think about how it would affect everybody else besides just himself. It was just a selfish decision."

But Lisa became a supportive partner, and she decided she would "go all in" as a key player in his campaign, even though campaigning was something she was wholly unfamiliar with.

Days later, the surprises began. Within hours of filing, he received a call from an employee union requesting a meeting. He had no idea what they wanted to discuss, nor that he was completely unprepared for the hostility he would experience.

Additionally, he and Lisa quickly realized they weren't prepared for people's comments on social media or remarks made to his daughter about her dad. Lisa began to experience how people treated her differently in person and on social media. In person, they would smile at her, but on social media, they wrote horrible comments about Steve's decision and disparaged his qualifications for the school board. Their reality was completely turned upside down, and some of their community acquaintances were no longer friends. They felt totally unprepared for this change, and they had no one to turn to. They had to manage it as they went forward.

Steve and Ron are good friends, and they laughed about this after Steve shared his decision with Ron. But Steve not only didn't consult his wife ahead of his decision, but he also didn't check with Ron either. As a good friend, he had ready access to Ron, who had successfully campaigned multiple times and served in public office for 24 years. Ron knows the territory and the ropes, and he is always ready to share his insights with friends and talented newcomers.

Steve went into the campaign completely naïve. When he called then-San Jose Councilmember Ash

Kalra, his representative on the City Council, to let him know he was running, Ash congratulated him but warned him that no election is easy.

Steve dismissed Ash's warning because he figured that he was only running for a school board seat– "a smaller, less visible position." His response was, "How bad could it be?" Ash told him to call him after the election to tell him if he felt the same. Well, after the election, Steve realized exactly what Councilmember Kalra was trying to tell him, that there is no such thing as a "small, less visible" political office. In the end, Steve didn't win the school board seat, but his story serves as a reminder of why your family needs to be involved and how you need to make your decision to run for office with eyes wide open.

Supervisor Susan Ellenberg and her husband Steve shared with us their reflections on their joint decision when Susan first ran for a local school board and later for County Supervisor. They both knew their first joint priority was their children and Susan's desire to be a good mom.

Susan felt that to make a commitment to run for a political seat without the full support of your partner and every family member in your home is selfish. She recognized that both campaigning and serving would take a lot of time and money from other priorities.

Without having the full support of your family, the decision is mostly based on ego rather than a desire to make an impact. Susan and Steve both agree that your decision as a family says how serious you are about being a candidate.

Additionally, many political contributors know that a successful political career requires the whole family to be committed to public service. A former staff member of Ron's at Santa Clara County decided to run for city council in Southern California. He had a good idea of the challenges and work ahead, but he underestimated the need to have his spouse's support. Unfortunately, he surprised her, and she didn't support his decision and was not involved in his campaign.

The campaign quickly became a huge burden for them both. They were always thinking about their schedules, the immense time commitment and household disruption (yet another late dinner, yet more time away).

This candidate was courting an important, well-known, and well-connected donor who made it very clear he wanted to meet with both the candidate and his spouse before contributing.

Although this scenario was unusual, it tells us this donor may have had a negative experience when a spouse was not on board and became a drag on the campaign. Because of a reluctant spouse, this candidate lost a contribution and support from an influential donor.

Ultimately, he didn't win the campaign. But he told us that the loss came with a sigh of relief. He clearly understood he would not have been able to serve effectively without his family's support and risked peace in his personal life.

For former San Jose Councilmember Chappie Jones and his wife Kelli, running for office was something that had been on Chappie's mind for 20 years. Kelli jokes that she just wanted Chappie to finally decide to run or stop talking about it. So, with his wife's support, Chappie decided to run for city council.

But another important component of Chappie's support was their adult children. He had a conversation with them about the campaign, but also his expectations of how their behavior would now more visibly represent their father. They signed up, and the campaign became a family affair as Chappie's kids also walked precincts with their parents.

Santa Clara County Supervisor and former San Jose Councilmember Cindy Chavez admits she would love to advise would-be candidates to be bold and make the decision to run on their own. But she understands that solo boldness must take a back seat to the necessity for this decision to be made in partnership with spouse and family.

She and her husband, Mike Potter, who is also currently serving in elected office as a Santa Clara County Open Space Authority Board Member, had a mutual understanding, even when they were dating, that public service was important to them. When they decided together that Cindy would run for public office, they were both very much aligned. She says it's best for everyone that the spouse is all in from the beginning. There will be hard days in public office, and sharing the demands, frustrations, and triumphs with your partner keeps the burdens bearable.

What is the role your spouse (and/or family) wants to play in your campaign and public life?

An important conversation to have with your spouse and family is about their preferred roles in the campaign and thereafter. There are many possible answers to this question—on one hand, they can be active, visible advocates, surrogates, or they can be backstage, recharger, babysitters and huggers, reality checkers, researchers, etc. The answer that works for you, your spouse, and your families must be deliberately and continually discussed and rechecked as time moves on and conditions evolve. Your family should be your rock and your resource for success, but you can't take them for granted.

Guisselle was recently asked by a local mayor's spouse, "What were the expectations she needed to meet in her role as 'first lady'?" Guisselle's response was that the only expectations are those established between you and your partner. Generally, the public doesn't necessarily ask anything special of a political spouse, especially at the local level, but the office holder or candidate likely will.

Unless you are the spouse of the President or a governor, you won't have an office or team to support you, and you're on your own. For the most part, the community is mostly interested in the elected official unless something negative happens. Of course, constituents are delighted to see and meet spouses since they are an extension of the office holder and can help enhance a public image.

It's up to you. You can accompany your spouse to events, support them at home, or continue your separate lives and careers. But never forget your professional, personal, and family life is still in the goldfish bowl, and you always must integrate your choices into your spouse's public life.

Steve Ellenberg took a leave of absence from his law firm to walk precincts for his wife, Susan, when she ran for Santa Clara County Supervisor. He says he loved knowing he was one of the only spouses who was walking precincts, and he was committed to it. He knocked on approximately 15,000 doors, walking daily for nearly six months.

Because he had invested so much into Susan's campaign, he acknowledged that it was difficult to go back to his law firm while she continued with the exciting work of setting up her office and diving into her role as a newly elected supervisor. But he understood that he needed to be clear about his role; he accompanied her to events, occasionally represented her when needed, and served as her eyes and ears in their community.

Guisselle cautions political spouses from losing their personal identity to their spouses. It's inevitable that you will be identified as "the spouse," but this role will end at some point, and you'll still have a lot of your own life left. You need to maintain your own identity that supports your own personal and professional roles and growth. Having a spouse who knows who they are and what they want, who can articulate their values and goals, and can advocate for themselves will strengthen the partnership for both of you.

It's important to understand that family support and involvement, whatever that may look like, is crucial to the candidate's or elected official's mental and emotional well-being. Ron remembers his colleagues nervously checking their watches as meetings ran late…but why? He learned later that their spouses weren't fully supportive of their public service. You will have plenty of other pressures and public expectations to manage, and it can be a lonely experience. The last thing you need is for your home/personal life to add to that stress.

We recommend that the spouse speak to other political spouses before you jump in the race, just as the candidate speaks to many politicians. We encourage candidates to take your spouse along to some of those exploratory meetings or make it a double date with another office holder and their spouse in those exploratory conversations. Spouses are seldom asked about their experience; we're sure that they'd be happy to share what they have learned if you only ask.

Lesson 4. Be clear about the role your spouse (and/or family) wants to play in your public life. How will they support you?

During the campaign…

Your family members can be excellent additions to your campaign team, and they're the next best thing to the candidate himself knocking on a voter's front door. When Ron campaigned for the Santa Clara County Board of Supervisors, his father walked precincts almost every day for nearly a year. Three decades later, Ron still credits his election victory to his father, Bob Gonzales.

Chappie Jones credits his wife, Kelli, for helping him win his council seat. Although she was new to the campaign experience, Kelli served as his campaign treasurer (a vital role requiring competence and trust) and walked precincts daily. Chappie says that voters in his district tell him to this day that they voted for him because his wife had knocked on their door.

Campaign roles can vary, including walking precincts, dialing for dollars for campaign funds, coordinating volunteers, stuffing envelopes, delivering lawn signs, or attending campaign events. Everyone can be put to work on a campaign, but setting priorities, boundaries, and clear schedules will be essential to sanity and health.

Kelli Jones recommends the spouse and family reflect on the following two questions.

- Do you have thick skin? Your spouse may be attacked, so how will you manage that?

- What are you doing to prepare yourself for this next role?

She recognizes that campaigning for and serving in public office is completely different from any other profession. Your spouse will serve in a world where they must be managers, negotiators, communicators, and conciliators and where they need to learn how to form alliances and count votes to get anything done. You can provide a framework to support them and help keep them on track.

Furthermore, Kelli says to ask yourself, what do you want personally out of this experience? She asks, "Do you want to be the sidecar or the caboose?" Are you okay with your spouse getting all the spotlight? How will this decision impact your professional career?

Once your family member is in office...

For Guisselle, attending and supporting Ron at community activities as Mayor was important to both. This was in addition to her own full-time job and her other community activities and organizations. She believed it was important for Ron's brand to show he was fully supported by his spouse and family.

Their agreement was that she could "veto" her attendance at certain events, but Ron would say when there were some, he considered it essential for her to be there. When they felt it was necessary to have family accompany Ron, and Guisselle couldn't go, another of Ron's family members would attend with him.

Some examples of activities that Guisselle and Ron attended include-

- Formal events supporting key community organizations.

- Formal evening events where Ron had a role in the program.

- High-profile community activities on weekends, such as 9/11 commemoration, neighborhood clean-ups, holiday parades, and community/ethnic festivals.

- Candidate fundraising events.

- Major City-sponsored events such as the new City Hall ribbon cutting.

- Weekday events supporting local organizations;

- Occasional out-of-state or international travel for special events or conferences.

Kelli Jones admits that attending events wasn't necessarily something she enjoyed, especially because her husband would be bombarded by people wanting to talk to him, and she would be left on her own. The events she chose, or they agreed to, were perhaps fewer, but it felt like the right amount for her. Know your preferences, state them clearly, and stick to them. And find enjoyment in the spectacle.

Your elected spouse will often be recognized while in public. This will bleed into your personal life too. People want to meet your spouse, talk to them, and complain to them, whether at a public event or while you're shopping for groceries or picking up the drycleaning. This is a commonplace occurrence, and losing some of your anonymity is a cost of being in the public eye.

For Nadine and Doug Horner, the transition to supporting Doug in his role as a Livermore city council member came more naturally. Both had long served the community in various capacities, Doug as a planning commissioner and Nadine as CEO of the local chamber of commerce. Their previous experience attending events, meeting people, and juggling schedules helped them both adjust to the higher demands that came with public office.

Attending events together and "date nights" are not the same thing.

Going to public events together usually doesn't mean it's date night for both partners. Perhaps for some, it could be (we say sarcastically), but we wouldn't necessarily recommend it as a substitution.

Most likely, the elected official will be busy talking and listening to constituents. That means the spouse needs to be strong enough to either join in the conversation with strangers or find a way to "work the room" on their own or be okay just waiting for their spouse to finish the conversation.

At public events, the spouse will be interrupted–during meals, during the program, in the parking lot–as constituents want a piece of the official. It's not much of a date–that's when the focus should all be on the both of you, alone together.

Again, this is where having clarity around roles and expectations will be important. For both, it means compromising, understanding, and extending empathy to minimize resentment and miscommunication.

The spouse and family…more than just attending events.

The spouses' role can certainly be much more than just accompanying the elected spouse to events. How will they manage their own time? How will they manage their own personal and professional life next to their spouse's public elected role? There's no right or wrong answer here, and what we are proposing is a reflection so that both the office holder and spouse are clear on how they can support each other on this journey. Carmen Stone, wife of long-term elected official Larry Stone in Santa Clara County, advises spouses to keep three things in mind. One, support your spouse. If you love them, you want them to win and be successful, support them. Two, be your own self. Whatever your spouse does, continue to do whatever it is you enjoy doing. Lastly, enjoy the time your spouse is serving in elected office. She admits they've had lots of wonderful things that have come from her husband's service in public office. She says they've both had great experiences, and some not so great, but either way, she has enjoyed the experience and the ancillary benefits that come from their public service role.

Rich Gordon and his husband, Dennis McShane, talk about the importance of supporting each other in their respective careers. Rich jokes that when they first met, he had season tickets for the San Francisco 49ers and Denny had season tickets to the opera.

Rich is in public service; Denny is a physician. They have very different personal and professional interests, but they shared they were super clear about their communication, especially when Rich was away in Sacramento serving in the state legislature. Together, they defined their priorities around their careers and where they came together to support each other.

Everybody will have different ways of managing and supporting their spouse in their elected role.

As an empty-nester, Kelli Jones happily shared that with Chappie busy with his civic duties and her kids gone from home, she decided to add a new family member, and they adopted a dog, who offers unconditional love and attention to them both.

Nadine Horner decided that she would pursue an MBA while her husband served in his first term as a council member. She figured that his time on the city council would take him away from home a great deal, so this was an opportunity she had always wanted to take.

Nadine also shares how it was important for her to understand the issues that her husband would be voting on. She knew she was an extension of her husband's brand and public image, and understanding the issues would prepare her to inevitably answer questions from neighbors or community friends she would bump into. Additionally, during the weeks when Doug had to prepare for a council meeting and they had personal commitments that involved a lot of driving, she would drive to allow Doug to study the council agenda packet.

What about the children?

What about your children's role? Depending on their age, will you (as appropriate) take them to events with you, or can family help you watch them while you are attending meetings and events? How much will you want to share about your role and current events? What role will they have in your overall public service role? What about their privacy, especially in this day of intense social media attention?

Rosanne Faust, former Redwood City Councilmember, talks about first choosing non-elected public service roles that fit her family schedule. As her children grew, she was able to consider other more prominent roles such as councilmember. But she also didn't move forward with any public roles until she spoke to her children to get their support. Her former husband and she also had a custody agreement where she was able to have the children on days when she didn't have to attend council meetings.

We do see times changing, where more children are attending events with their elected parents. The children of Raul Peralez and Victoria Ramirez were born while Raul was on the city council. Raul would take his son, even as a baby, to many community events. That's a great icebreaker, and it provides a great reason to leave early. We also notice that current San Jose Mayor Matt Mahan takes his young children to community events, which is a tremendous learning opportunity for them.

Letitia Clark also took her children to events and even city council meetings. She jokes that they would do their homework while the council meeting was in session, and that helped them to hone their skill to focus while ignoring the crowds and noise from the meeting. Their attendance exposed them to what "Mommy was doing" in the community. She was proud that the community always commented on how well-behaved they were.

There is no one-size-fits-all model that works for every family. If you do decide to take your children to community events, we caution you to have someone help you watch the children, especially for younger kids. Hopefully, they are also well-behaved, so they are neither a distraction nor an embarrassment to you or the community. Like it or not, your children and their behavior are an extension of your public image, and the public is always quick to judge.

Cindy Chavez and Mike Potter chose not to take their son to many events. Looking back now, they say they could have explained more to their son about current events or negative headlines about his mother. At the time, they felt protecting him from the negativity that came with the job was more important. They reflect on how they could have done better to help him understand what was happening so that he wouldn't worry.

For other children, it may be a loss of anonymity that may be of concern. Susan and Steve Ellenberg share that their youngest daughter has felt that her name recognition is both a blessing and a burden. She works for the County, and she finds that her colleagues recognize her last name and immediately connect her to her elected mother.

Although their daughter and other children were all on board with their mother's public service, Steve and Susan shared that their daughter was concerned about building her own personal brand separate from her mother's as she embarked on her own professional career.

Guilt about the amount of time spent away from home is a universal theme expressed by our elected parents and spouses. Ron remembers the guilt he felt about missing key moments with his three young daughters.

Years later, he asked his oldest daughter, Miranda, how she felt, and her response was, "Dad, we knew that when you weren't home, it was because you were serving the community and not out partying or something like that." That brought some solace and a chuckle to Ron, but he admits he still feels some guilt for not having been there more for them.

Dave Cortese, currently a California State Senator, started his public service at a young age. He learned through time and experience what he could have done differently as a parent involved deeply in public service. He remembers being in meetings, watching each minute tick by, thinking about what his four children were doing at that very moment, and feeling he was missing out on their lives. Even though he tried not to think about it, it was always a haunting feeling that plagued him during those long meetings.

He never shared this feeling with his children. Dave learned along the way that some of his children were more sensitive than others, and they needed to hear him tell them how hard it was and the struggles he faced being away from the family. With his wife, Patti, he found that it would have been wiser to include their children in their discussions and decisions about running for office.

They both realized their children would have preferred to have had a voice in these decisions. They both said that they now see how campaigning and politics made their children feel "like they were the old shoe in the dryer, just bouncing around." Just like your voters and your constituents, your kids and your spouse want to be consulted. They want to be heard about important matters.

Consider how your public life will affect your children's lives, which will vary depending on their age. Especially if your children are older, you should listen to their questions and concerns, and you need to prepare them for how they respond to people's comments in school or in the news.

When one of Dave and Patti's daughters was in the 7th grade, her teacher recognized her last name and asked if her father was running for San Jose mayor. When the girl said yes, the teacher told her that he did not vote for her father. Their daughter was really affected and embarrassed by her teacher's comment.

Dave recognizes now that this situation might have been avoided if they had prepared their children, or even their teachers, with better communication. Now he sees that for a child with a parent in politics, it may be like growing up without full-time parents. You need to pay close attention to how your child processes their emotions so that you can support them effectively.

Whether you are the candidate or office holder, or a family member, you each play an important but different role that must be understood by all of you. Your family's support is invaluable to the mental and emotional well- being of anyone who desires to serve or currently serves in elected office, and you cannot take it for granted.

Chapter 1 Summary of Lessons:

Lesson 1: You and your partner need to understand that running for elected office and serving in public office will never follow a normal 9-5 schedule.

Lesson 2: Do opposition research on yourself.

Lesson 3: Don't decide to run for office without speaking first to your spouse and family.

Lesson 4: Be clear about the role your spouse wants to play in your public life.

CHAPTER 2

What's Your "Why?"

"Serving in public office was a great honor and privilege. Elected leaders are stewards of time and place. Helping others, building community, and impacting the future..."
-Rich Gordon, former California State Assemblymember

Even the most experienced candidate may lose sight of people's true motivations and be disappointed by the lack of follow-through in their political support. Those moments may hurt, but we hope you seek solace and anchor yourself in your "why" and what is driving you to serve in public office.

Lesson 5. Remember that if you are being courted to run, never assume that these same leaders will be with you, volunteer, contribute, and work as hard as you need them to help you win.

You will quickly find out whom you can count on and whom you can't. People may appear enthusiastic about your candidacy, but that doesn't always translate into active and practical support. As Steve Guerrero found out early in his school board campaign, the people who had encouraged him to run didn't show up to raise funds, walk precincts, or make phone calls on his behalf.

Also, you can't assume that because someone endorsed you on one campaign, they will endorse you on another one. Every campaign is unique, the issues of the day change, the field of opposing candidates is different, and you may have more baggage to account for.

Ron is steadfast in this rule of thumb: within the first 24 hours of your campaign announcement, you should have 100 supporters you are 90 percent confident will make an early donation for the maximum amount allowed.

Give yourself time to prepare your real foundation of support, and don't just jump in the race because you've been recruited. Build your base of volunteers ahead to help with the campaign so that the burden doesn't fall solely on your family. Know your likely opposition, understand why they're running, and gauge what their support realistically looks like.

Your full-time job, your civic role, personal nances, and real or apparent con icts

Here's another place for doing your homework: A spouse's or family member's job could become a conflict of interest during and/or after the campaign. Cross check with their place of employment to identify potential conflicts if you win the election and develop ways to resolve them long before you might be called upon to explain them.

For example, if your family member receives or seeks public contracts, that could be a conflict of interest. Potential conflicts of interest are not insurmountable, but this is another reminder of the importance of doing opposition research on yourself and being ready to respond to the possibility of being targeted for the work that you, your spouse, or your family do. You might need to consult an attorney knowledgeable about public process and ethics to help guide you through this thicket.

Another important question you need to consider is how you will manage your regular day job while running a campaign and caring for your family. Unless your public service is in a large city, county, or state office, most locally elected positions are part-time. You will likely need to maintain a full-time outside job and serve as a part-time elected official. When Ron served on the Sunnyvale City Council, he needed to maintain his full-time job at the Hewlett-Packard (HP) Company.

Managing your civic duties while balancing your time and commitments with your full-time job and family is a complex challenge that you need to think through. Work with your employer to understand employee policies, explore possible conflicts, and gain employer support for your decision.

Your campaign and civic duties may require as much time as your full-time job. Having the understanding and support from your employer can make managing all these responsibilities much easier for you and your family. Fortunately for Ron, he had the full support of his employer, HP, which was a model "corporate citizen" that encouraged its employees to be engaged in their communities. You might be lucky that way, or maybe not–it's best to find out sooner than later.

Lesson 6. Do you have the time and money to run a campaign?

Before launching your campaign, ask yourself and answer these questions:

- What kind of support or resources do you have to manage your day job responsibilities?

- What kind of support or resources do you have to manage your family responsibilities?

- Does your current job offer the flexibility you will need to campaign or serve?

Some candidates can keep their full-time jobs, others can hedge their bet and take a leave of absence, and some choose to quit their jobs. Chappie Jones made the decision to leave his job at Apple so he could focus entirely on his campaign, but he was in a financial position to be able to do that.

If you can swing it, taking a leave of absence could help you concentrate on your new political demands. It also keeps the door open if you don't win the election.

- If you don't have time to raise funds, do you have personal wealth to help fund the campaign if necessary?

Doug Horner, former City of Livermore Councilmember, is part of a very small minority of elected officials who never faced an opponent for both of his elections. It was the first time in the 125 years of his city's history there was an uncontested city council seat. This simplified life for Doug, and he and his wife Nadine were relieved they didn't have to ask for political donations.

In fact, they had decided to use personal funds for campaign expenses if someone decided to run against Doug. They felt that asking for donations in a small community would lead them to feel that they "owed" something to those donors, even though most community campaign donors don't expect such a relationship. However, running unopposed is an extremely rare occurrence, and it is much more likely that fundraising will be a major component of your campaign.

Here are some basic considerations regarding financing your campaign:

- How much money do you need to raise to win?

- Will you really make the time to prioritize fundraising?

- Do you have the confidence and nerve to ask people for their money? And are you good with hearing rejections?

- Do you have a donor base that will help fund your initial campaign fundraising?

- Are you ninety percent certain that you have at least one hundred people who would donate the maximum contribution amount by the first fundraising deadline?

If you're not comfortable asking for money, or if you don't have a solid base of support, running for office may be something that you want to reconsider. Your objective at the beginning of any campaign election is to be the number one fundraiser for the first fundraising filing period, and this will require time, commitment, strategy, and genuine support.

You may be disappointed with friends or family that you may think will donate to your campaign, and then they don't. Or may have the financial capacity to give more, and they don't. This is something we've heard from several of our interviewees. It may be a reality you'll have to face once you start your fundraising efforts.

Santa Clara County Supervisor Susan Ellenberg and her husband Steve both agree that they should have put more of their own money into her campaign so they didn't incur campaign debt that became a burden carried over after the election. Susan also advised that you should not waste people's time and money if you're not serious and not willing to do the hard work. And that means making some tough decisions at the beginning of how much time, effort, and resources you will put into your campaign.

Public service is a vocation not a career

Lesson 7. Public service and running for office should be viewed as a vocation: It is a privilege to serve.

We believe that public service is a vocation focused on helping other people. Once you begin looking at elected service as a full-time career rather than as a passion for serving, you may start making decisions that are based on the fear of losing your elected position and not on the common good for all you serve.

Be honest with yourself. As you consider running for elected office, we encourage you to think about how you are connected to your self-awareness–spiritually, emotionally, physically, and cognitively.

You will be making decisions on issues on which you may not have any expertise, such as land use, finance and budget, labor relations, police violence, infrastructure–and, most recently, managing the local impact of a global pandemic. You will be making critically important decisions that will challenge your personal philosophy, values, and morals, and these votes will materially affect the quality of lives and livelihoods of the people who elected you. How will you make decisions that walk the line between individual rights and the larger public good? How will you sort out the truth from the clamor of the noisiest voices?

Once you've made your decision, will you be able to place your head on your pillow and be able to sleep because you are comfortable with your vote?

Most of us don't understand what this means until you are charged with making decisions such as:

- A long-time campaign supporter and contributor's development project is coming to a vote, but for many reasons, the project doesn't fit your land use goals. What will you do? Vote for it? Face your supporter, tell them why you aren't voting for it, and take a chance that you will lose their future support?

- When it's time to cut the budget, you are faced with hard choices, such as continuing to fund tuberculous shots for kids or continuing to fund drug and alcohol rehabilitation services for adults?

- A small group of your school district's voters object to your teachers talking about the Holocaust without indicating that there is a belief the Holocaust is a product of "fake news." What's your position and how will you defend it?

- When the meeting room is full of angry people who are urging you to "protect their property values" by not approving an affordable housing project in their neighborhood that you believe is essential, can you stand up to them and tell them you support the project?

You may have an idea of what the office you are seeking entails. For example, for a city, you might be voting on zoning and land use, streetlights and potholes, graffiti and playgrounds.

But the reality is that all politics is local—and personal. There is no issue that is off topic because everything affects local government. National, state, and regional issues intersect and end up landing on the local level. Here are just a few public policy areas that Ron voted on over 24 years of public service that most people would not consider local government issues:

- Censorship in public libraries

- Civil rights

- Abortion

- Same sex marriage

- Provision of city health benefits to same sex partners/spouses

- Gun control

- Individual property rights vs. public good (public condemnation of private property)

- Building affordable and higher density housing to meet regional housing needs and goals.

Get honest with yourself. What's your "why?"

Many people view a political seat as a job, and it shouldn't be viewed that way. Again, we believe it should be viewed as a vocation; it's a calling to a higher purpose.

Why? We have witnessed the major distinction when decisions are made by someone who views their position as their day job and someone who views it as a calling for service. If it's merely your day job, you will tend to make decisions based on not losing your job, thus motivated by fear. And fear-based decisions can often lead to mental torment and professional disaster.

If you know your "why," if you know your principles for service, then you can make better decisions for the people you are serving.

Lesson 8. Be honest with yourself and understand what guides and drives you to run for office.

You need to answer the following questions before you take the leap into a campaign.

- What guides you? What are your governing principles?

  Self-awareness of who you are, what you stand for, and what guides you will be your foundation and compass as you make key public policy decisions. Your foundation needs to be in place and understood before you decide to run. This will require you to display a level of honesty with yourself about difficult and controversial matters that you may have never had to deal with before.

- Start by asking yourself questions, without self-judgment, about why you want to run for this elected position.

  Is it from your ego self-satisfaction? Is it the potential power and/or influence that you think you will gain? Or is it for the impact that you can make in your community? What do you care most about? Why?

Your answers will help you weigh your decision about running for an elected position and the tradeoffs for you and your family. You will be making sacrifices of time, resources, frustrations, and privacy when you pursue public service, and there will be rewards of accomplishment and partnership as well. You need to understand what your North Star is before you make such a big commitment.

You will be asked these questions throughout your campaign and while serving in elected office: "Why are you running? What is your vision?" Your answers will come directly from your experience, your self-examination, and your values learned from your family and role models. They will clarify your reason to run, drive your campaign message, and keep you motivated when challenges and obstacles show up.

You want to see a political candidate who couldn't answer this question? Let's go back into history. Search on the internet, "Ted Kennedy: Why do you want to be President?" In 1979, Senator Kennedy was interviewed on live television by CBS Reporter Roger Mudd who asked this essential question: "Why do you want to be President" (CBS 17, 202).

Kennedy's response was hesitant, incoherent, and without a message. Historians point to that moment and his lack of self-awareness and his inability to even articulate why he wanted to be President was the turning point and end of his campaign. Thus, in one short interview, Kennedy's ambition to be President was ended.

If your "why" is important enough to you and is worth the sacrifice, then you will have something to fall back on when you're inevitably faced with the difficulties that come with campaigning for and holding public office. From the start, you will be making decisions that affect the public good, and so what principles will guide you as you make public votes?

Many times, over his 24 years of public service Ron was faced with a council chamber filled with voters vocally opposed to something he was proposing or supporting. He has shared that he had often thought about all the voters who weren't in the room and how his decisions would affect them and the entire community he was elected to serve.

Ron has always been very clear about his "why." His father, Bob Gonzales, was his hero and role model who taught his five children an important principle. He would say, "Every one of us, in some way, in your own way, has a responsibility to improve the lives of others."

Bob Gonzales demonstrated that principle in his own life. As life-time truck driver and union member, he would rush home after a long day of work, eat a quick dinner, shower, and head off to a community meeting to organize and advocate for community improvement. He often took Ron with him to activities where Ron saw first-hand how people working together can make a huge differ-ence– and that effective leadership is essential.

Among the many events he attended, Ron fondly remembers joining union picket lines as a teenager– including United Farm Workers Union grape and lettuce boycotts led by Cesar Chavez, and when a labor strike closed the entrance to San Fran-cisco International Airport.

Ron distinctly remembers the notion of public service first came to him when as a youth, he accompanied his father, Bob, to a local school board meeting. Bob was advocating for the hiring of more ethnically diverse teachers, and Ron was angered when he saw the school board members not paying attention to the public speakers, including his father. He thought to himself, "this is not the way the government is supposed to work."

Chappie Jones reminded us that self-awareness is critically important when you make your decision to run and serve. "The campaign is extremely difficult. It challenges your relationship with yourself and your spouse, and it challenges your self-esteem and whole sense of self because you're frequently attacked."

He recommends asking yourself the hard questions about what is driving you to take on this challenge. If your answer is because you like being the center of attention, or that you are doing this for your own resume, then Chappie would advise you to "don't do it." But if you "really want to serve the community, try to make the world and your community a better place, then go for it" --especially if you have a clear idea of what you want to achieve in office.

The ego is one factor, but it shouldn't be the only one.

Now, let's be realistic. Many of our life and career decisions are made based on ego. It's no different for candidates and office holders. Ego, which might be a stand in for self-confidence, isn't necessarily a bad thing; we all seek respect and a sense of accomplishment.

Santa Clara County Assessor Larry Stone, who has nearly a half century in public service, said a strong ego can be helpful when you're enduring negative comments and harsh scrutiny. But he also said it should only be one of many factors, and certainly not the most important to seeking public office.

Ultimately the ego factor is superficial. When things get tough, you need to call upon your core values, your "why," to keep yourself on track, manage discouragement, and make good decisions. Those who look to public service to satisfy their need for power and accolades will find quickly that is not enough; that's when the job becomes a trap, not a vocation.

Ron remembers a local official who was termed out of a state office a few years ago and wanted to seek (yet again) a local elected office. Ron asked this person why she wanted to seek public office once again. And the candid answer was, "because I miss the power." The candidate's campaign was not successful. Voters and donors usually can see through an ego-driven candidate. Or maybe it's just karma.

Supervisor Susan Ellenberg reminded us that it's also just an election. It's not a hill to die on. If you don't win but know your "why," you can do other things with your life to make a positive difference in your community. If power and attention are your drivers, it's likely you will start contorting yourself to please your audiences, compromising your values, or changing your brand. That is the beginning of a downward spiral. Susan said she encourages people to be willing to win, but also to know that they can live with losing and still accomplish good. Winning at any cost is a dangerous line to cross.

Before Cindy Chavez was elected as a Santa Clara County Supervisor, she served on the San Jose City Council. Cindy shared that she was prompted to run for council after she and her husband Mike Potter experienced random gunshots fired in their neighborhood and at their home. But that was only the prompt; Cindy's desire to serve came from a deeper source, her exposure to social justice from her church.

California State Assemblymember Ash Kalra was born in India and raised in Canada and the U.S. He recalled he first thought of helping others when he was child and had visited India. He saw the extreme poverty in India, and he remembered feeling a conscious calling and sense of obligation to help others. Ultimately, he decided to run for the

San Jose City Council after serving on city commissions and working for the local District Attorney's office.

Santa Clara County Assessor Larry Stone grew up in a Seattle political family, and his father once campaigned, unsuccessfully, for Congress. He fondly remembers as a young boy of nine accompanying his father to the local Lockheed shipyards to leaflet union workers for candidates his dad was supporting. Much later Larry attended a Sunnyvale City Council meeting and was disgusted at a council member who was very condescending towards members of the public.

That led him to becoming involved in a community government reform group, and the next step was his first successful city council campaign. Public service for Larry was a logical progression stemming from his upbringing and his civic engagement.

Doug and Nadine Horner in Livermore, CA, chose different paths toward public service. They both wanted to get involved in their community, but she became a business leader, and he pursued city politics. Doug was first appointed to a seat on the Livermore City Council and then ran for it two years later. Those two years as an appointed member had

prepared him to campaign and serve, and to understand deeply what he could accomplish.

Former California State Assemblymember
Rich Gordon learned the lesson of public service
from his grandmother who would cook a pot of
stew every day and put it on the front porch so
local unemployed men could have something to
eat. Public service was ingrained in him as a child; it
meant that if you had something to give, you gave
it away. This led him into ministry with the United
Methodist Church, and then into social work for 20
years. Finally, Rich entered local politics to advance
his goals for service–a shared family vision since
one of his sisters is a nurse and another is a public
guardian with the county.

Tustin, CA City Councilmember, Letitia Clark,
was inspired to lead when she served as a staff
member for a New Orleans City Councilmember
during hurricane Katrina. She saw how elected officials and city staff responded to the natural disaster
with genuine compassion and commitment when
communities needed local government to really
work for people.

After this experience Leticia felt she had a better
sense of what it meant to serve, especially during a
crisis, and she knew she would do it herself. Later
as Mayor of Tustin, both during COVID-19 pan-

demic and after the George Floyd protests, she felt her time in New Orleans after Hurricane Katrina prepared her to lead under difficult and stressful conditions.

Knowing your "why" even applies to courtship in the public eye. Victoria Ramirez and Raul Peralez's courtship started early in Raul's political career when he was running for San Jose City Council. Along with learning to navigate life in a campaign, he was also learning how to navigate his new relationship with Victoria. Now that he was in the fishbowl, people would share their opinions of what he should or shouldn't do with his personal life, including whom he should or should not date. That included whether he should be dating Victoria. When Raul talked to Victoria about this, she told him clearly, "If you're going to let them tell you who you can and cannot date before you're even elected, then you don't deserve the seat."

It's easy to be buffeted by too many opinions about what will benefit your campaign or your political future, but you need to be able to take a stand if you want to stay true to yourself and your values. Again, knowing your "why" will help you stay grounded and clear about what is authentic.

Life, both in general and in politics, always has highs and lows. The highs may include garnering positive attention and accolades from your community for your actions and words, getting the votes you need to pass policy; and seeing the tangible impacts your decisions have had on your community.

But there will be those days when you have to say no to your friends; you don't get the votes to pass your policy ideas; you get pounded by the media or your colleagues may keep you grounded because of lack of support. How do you keep moving forward when the days are darkest?

Cindy Chavez said that political consultants always tell the candidate to write down all the things they want to accomplish when they run for office. But she's never been asked to write down her deep reasons for running for office. She has learned over many campaigns and years of service that knowing your "why" makes everything else easier in the role. Understanding your core values will be your compass to navigate through the sometimes-rocky waters of political life.

In summary, you need to anchor yourself with your values, your goals, your desired legacy– your "why" for public service. All that you do after taking office should be connected to your why.

Chapter 2 Summary of Lessons:

Lesson 5: If you are being courted to run, never assume that these same leaders will be with you during the campaign.

Lesson 6: Do you have the time and money to run a campaign?

Lesson 7: Public service and running for office should be viewed as a vocation.

Lesson 8: Be honest with yourself and understand what guides and drives you to run for office.

CHAPTER 3

You've Won, Now What?

Bill McKay (portrayed by actor Robert Redford in the 1972 film "The Candidate"), candidate for Senate, pulls off his upset victory, and he's immediately surrounded by celebration, press coverage, and congratulatory speeches. When he steals a moment alone in his hotel room on election night, McKay is left silent. The realization that he doesn't actually have the slightest idea how to accomplish his campaign promises sets in, and he asks Lucas, his campaign consultant "...so what do we do now?" (Gaughan, 2022; Pascoe, 2009).

"The best day in a mayor's term is election night." -Henry Cisneros, former Mayor of San Antonio, Texas, and Secretary of the U.S. Department of Housing and Urban Development

Welcome to elected office

Winning an election can be one of your proudest moments, and at the same time one filled with terror. "To whom much is given, much is expected," and with the responsibility of an elected position come many expectations, some you may be aware of and some not so much.

There is no onboarding process. There is no playbook of what to do first. There is no "Idiot's Guide" to public office. There's no new employee orientation for a newly elected official.

You should already have a sense of your top priorities and what you campaigned on. But now you need to learn about this organization you're joining, its past, current and future public policy issues, its resources in terms of funding, people and talent, and reputation, and institutional procedures, protocols, and culture. And of course, you need to become well acquainted with your other elected colleagues who will be crucial to your ability to accomplish your policy goals.

This is all "on-the-job training," learning as you go, but Lesson 9 offers some advice for you to organize your onboarding.

But first, two quick tips for your family's onboarding…

One, you will want to keep your tax dollars local. All of you should do as much as practical to shop locally, which sends a clear message to your constituents that you are part of your community, and you are doing your part to generate local sales tax revenue for your agency. From now on, while you serve in office, most of your family's shopping, restaurant and entertainment spending should stay where you serve.

Guisselle remembers her girlfriends would want to go to dinner outside of San Jose, and she would always have Ron's "little voice" pop up reminding her that it would be important to keep her tax dollars at home. Another spouse of a local mayor told her that her partner would remind her of the same thing.

And two, your spouse and family now will be subjected to community members and friends asking you for access to your newly elected spouse. You will need to find a graceful way of handling these requests—our recommendation is that you should be ready to provide a reliable official contact they can email or call. This contact will vary with the size and nature of your agency, but having an effective and appropriate way of handling the public while you're out and about is truly important for the reputation of you and your spouse.

Of course, you must show genuine empathy and interest to your spouse's constituents since you too now represent "City Hall." We suggest you define boundaries around these requests, otherwise, you will be fielding resident issues that should be done by the government professionals.

Lesson 9. Once you're in office, understand that you don't know everything.

Be intentional about figuring out what it is that you don't know and reach out to those people inside and outside of the organization who do know, and who have institutional history with the public policy issues and your jurisdiction.

Ask yourself these questions:

- What are my top three priorities for my elected office? We recommend you begin to picture what you will promote as your successes in your re-election brochure.

- Think about who you need to include to help you accomplish these goals, both individuals and groups.

- Establish a work plan for accomplishing goals. This will provide a starting place, and it will be continually revised as you learn the ropes.

- If you have office staff, how does your staff play a role in achieving your priorities? Or if you are a part-time elected official, how can the organization management and community stakeholders help you better understand how to move forward.

- Are your predecessor and their staff willing to provide you with onboarding guidance? Can you rehire their team members to help you get started?

- And, first and foremost, you should reach out to the organization's nonpolitical staff for briefings and tours to become more familiar with the issues, services, and community from their professional perspective. Staff members are experts–retain your humility to learn from them.

Below are set of sample questions you can ask your organization staff:

- Who do you need to work with to get your priorities accomplished?

- How often will/should you meet with organizational/department leaders to monitor progress on your priorities?

- What are the hot buttons within the organization, and for the community?

By setting your priorities and sharing them, you can provide a foundation for collaboration between you and organizational staff.

But please understand that, generally, your organization's staff and managers don't work for you as one elected official. They work for the chief administrator, who works for you and your elected colleagues collectively. Building genuine relationships with staff is about learning, mutual respect, and collaboration—but you have decidedly different roles.

- Who are your go-to contacts for each department? This may not be the department head, but instead, a middle-level manager who knows how to navigate the bureaucracy to assist you.

- Who else in the organization/community can assist you in achieving your priorities?

- Which elected colleagues can you count on for wise and practical advice?

Additionally, you should seek out past office holders for their history, ideas, and experience. You can also establish informal advisory committees from different interests in your community to provide you with direct insight as to how your constituents feel and perceive the issues.

So, when thinking about how to involve the community in your onboarding and future collaboration, consider the following questions:

- What do you want your community to do and how can they help you?

- What can you ask them to do? Remember, if you don't ask, they don't know you need their help.

- Establish close relationships with community/groups, neighborhood associations, etc. where you don't have to attend their meetings all the time. Close relationships will allow staff to be the key contact, and you can attend the meetings, based on your schedule.

- Does your office have a database of supporters, neighborhood/community leaders/associations?

- How can you use that database to communicate with them on your priorities and for you to listen to them?

- What kind of communication plan is in place to keep in touch with your database?

- How can outside organizations (policy, private sector, nonprofits, etc.) help you accomplish your priorities?

- How can social media help your office connect to your community?

Sometimes candidates lower their antenna once they get into office. Winning the campaign is only the first step, however. The real work is yet to come. Once you're in office, keep your antenna raised, seek out people inside and outside your organization to get your questions answered, and always stay curious.

How do I handle the politics of serving?

"If you think it's a requirement, and it's drudgery, then you shouldn't be in office." -Larry Stone, Santa Clara County Assessor

Lesson 10. Manage your schedule. Manage your priorities. Manage your office.

Manage your schedule.

As we mentioned in Lesson 1, an elected office doesn't follow a 9-to-5 schedule. So, what can you do to set boundaries that will give you time for yourself and your family? We highly recommend you set aside at least one day a week for yourself, and a day of rest for your staff is also a good idea. As mayor, Ron also liked two nights off from weekday evening events. Your restricted days and evenings should be well known by your staff—and your family, too, especially if you don't have staff. This will also help your team prioritize meetings and events. Again, it's no joke: you could go to meetings and events every day and every night of your public career if you let demand drive your schedule.

Your office should have a scheduling system accessible to groups who wish to request your presence at events and meetings. The days you reserve for yourself should be blocked out in your system so that the community is aware of your schedule availability and restrictions. You should develop criteria for when your rule can be broken.

Ron's office rule was if the event had a citywide, state, or national impact, then there could be an exception made for working on those "days off." The more consistent you are about your scheduling priorities, the more the community and your colleagues will know and come to respect your boundaries.

The amount of time you stay at events also sends a message to the community. Spending your entire evening at one event rather than giving people only a few minutes at numerous events says, "You are important enough for me to give you my entire evening." This gesture can help build stronger trust and rapport with that part of your community.

On the other hand, dropping by an event for only a few minutes because you are trying to squeeze many stops in one evening says, "You're not important enough to me to stay and I'm doing you a favor by merely waving the flag." How you manage your schedule can be a clear signal about your priorities for serving your constituencies.

Managing your schedule means managing yourself, including making your self-care a priority. All too often, self-care becomes a luxury in the face of stress and the demands on your time, and it becomes one of the first things we give up.

How many times have we given up going to the gym, or taking a daily walk, just to get an extra few minutes at the office or to attend one more "important" event? When we are doing our most difficult work is when we need to maintain the structures in our lives that remind us of who we are and keep us mentally and emotionally healthy.

Manage your priorities.

Being clear about your priorities is both beneficial and essential, if you have 100 priorities, you have no priorities. We recommend you have only three to five top priorities that you can focus your time and attention on. They can be priority buckets for related matters, but they will keep you on track to achieve your goals.

However, be aware that once you take office you will be quickly overwhelmed with issues that you never knew existed. You will find many other projects and issues that will be waiting for you in your inbox, left on your doorstep, or thrust in your face. Those issues may include unfinished public policy issues still in progress or need decisions; community demands that also need decisions; other organizational priorities that will require decisions; burning issues of the day across the nation or in the world that beg for your response, and the general day-to-day constituent service and relationships.

You shouldn't confuse those priorities with your own agenda, as important and as necessary it is for you to find a way to deal with them. Without your sustained focus on your goals, you can be easily overwhelmed by the pressure of matters outside your own agenda.

Additionally, other elected officials will seek and even demand your support for their issues, which is a natural part of politics. But stay focused! It will be very easy to be distracted by what we call "squirrel moments" triggered by the needs of others in and outside the organization.

Obviously, you need to respect colleagues but find other ways to address their needs. This could involve your staff, if you have staff, or understanding how your colleagues can help you with your priorities too. If you are clear about your agenda, you will be able to make decisions on other issues that come to you, with a more discerning perspective.

Why only three to five priorities? Because it's easier for you, and more importantly, for your constituents and colleagues, to remember what's important to you—to the voters.

This is especially important if you lead large government organizations. Department heads and management will observe how disciplined you are with your priorities and how your vision will set the agenda for the organization. Guisselle recalls a city worker telling her after one of Ron's annual State of the City addresses, "I always look forward to the Mayor's State of City addresses because he always gives us a clear outline for our city's priorities."

However, also remember this: whatever you seek to achieve, it may take years to accomplish, even going past your time in office. Be careful what you say about your priorities because both the public and the media will measure your success by the goals you articulated.

Recently elected Mayor of San Jose, Matt Mahan, articulated his four priorities during an election night speech for his first 100 days in office. They included reducing homelessness, strengthening public safety, tackling blight, and economic development. Worthy and clear and ambitious goals, but he will learn that solving those issues will likely take his entire tenure as mayor– if he is lucky.

Having a high bar for achievement is fine, but it also invites more scrutiny for evaluating success.

As Chicago architect and city planner, Daniel Burnham said more than a century ago, "Make no little plans; they have no magic to stir men's blood and probably themselves will not be realized. Make big plans; aim high in hope and work, remembering that a noble, logical diagram once recorded will never die."

Early in his political career, Ron was adamant about extending the Bay Area Rapid Transit system to San Jose and Silicon Valley. With commitment, discipline, and continuing support from his successors and stakeholders, it has taken 30 years to finally realize this project after countless meetings, debates, studies, and elections.

When you are clear with yourself and your constituencies about the political realities and budget constraints, support, and time, you still can make genuine progress to big goals despite the slow wheels of government policymaking. Let your organization and your colleagues know what your priorities are. Schedule regular meetings with leaders and managers so they understand your agenda and how they can help you achieve it.

Manage your of ce

If you have an office with staff to set up, here are some ideas for organizing it. Your team should play three key roles for you:

1) Your team should be a complement for where you may have weaknesses, need more knowledge, or even balance with your personality. For example, if you are an introvert, make sure that some team members have an extrovert personality that can help you interact with constituents.

2) Your staff are a vital part of your support system. You can count on them to help get the day-to-day work done for your organization and community.

3) Staff members are your "brand ambassadors." They represent you and your office, your priorities, and you as a person. Their words and actions also reflect on you, so they too should have a desire to serve the public and have their own "why."

Hiring a good team is important, for they are your extensions. Just as your job is not easy, so is theirs; they will have to endure public criticism, have unusual work hours, and be able to achieve balance in their lives while becoming experts in their assigned policy and service areas.

Where you'll spend your time.

If you serve as a city councilmember, a huge portion of responsibilities include land use decisions. However, many newcomers are unfamiliar with land use policies and issues. If you have staff, you should hire someone with solid land use experience. If you are a part-time official, then ask city management for a comprehensive orientation. You also can pursue training from organizations such as the League of California Cities or California State Association of Counties.

As you establish your office think about the following:

- What are your office operating protocols, such as: how do you handle constituents and colleagues; how do you respond to scheduling requests; how will you stay visible in your community?

- How will you maintain a professional image for your office? For example, this can range from having an office dress code to setting standards for response times for constituent communications.

- How will you manage scheduling requests? Here are some scheduling guidelines to help you stay focused.

  o What is my purpose for attending?

  o Does your participation help advance your priorities?

  o How can we maximize social media to boost visibility before, during, and after events?

  o How can community members feel special or heard?

  o Who will be at the event who might be able to help achieve your goals?

If you manage your own schedule, then most likely you're a part-time elected official, and thus "an office of one." Meaning you don't have any staff to help you manage the influx of scheduling requests. So, to keep your sanity, it's just as important that you ask yourself the same type of questions.

As a part-time elected official, Letitia Clark has two full-time jobs: her day job as a marketing communications professional and her elected role. That's not counting her role as a wife and mother of two children.

In her "part-time" job, she can spend up to 60 hours per week in many meetings, attending events, and preparing for council meetings. Her day job accounts for another 60 hours per week.

She's learned to be very clear about her priorities for her time. She says you must enjoy reading (especially endless council agendas and staff reports), and you must find things that boost your energy and allow you to do the hard and important things.

Leticia's family has adjusted to her time constraints, but when she's with family, she makes sure it's quality time, and she makes it a point of not being distracted with any work—no multitasking allowed! Her children have attended council meetings and events with her so they can see what she's doing in the community and spend some time together.

Through their experience together, she was inspired to write a children's book titled *"Mommy is the Mayor"* to explain to both kids and adults how a city is run, how decisions are made, and how they can support their communities.

Manage your schedule. Manage your priorities. Manage your office. These build a structure to keep you from being overwhelmed by distractions, the flood of information, stress, and temptations. A structure where you can find solace, dependability, and discipline to help you succeed and thrive.

While we don't cover personal branding in this book, we highly recommend you explore the concept and how it might apply to your pursuit of public service. Your personal brand is both your unique combination of skills, experiences, and personality that make you who you are, and how you present yourself to the world. Effective personal branding can differentiate you from the pack and allow you to build trust and opportunities with prospective clients, employers, colleagues, and the public.

Conscious and deliberate personal branding is the process of creating and promoting an authentic identity for yourself. As a public official, you can shape it by how you handle your schedule, your office, and your priorities. It's influenced by the consistency of your messaging, and your presence both online and offline. Your staff and their actions and words are a component of your personal brand.

There are plenty of resources on the subject. We recommend starting by reading Guisselle's book, *Take Charge of Your Brand.*

Anchor yourself

As with many high-profile professional positions, it's all too easy to confuse yourself with your role. Your colleagues or team members may treat you as if where you sit is who you are. You want to be authentic, but your highly visible role shouldn't define who you are as a person. Your elected position is merely an activity, not your essence, but the spotlight and attention on you in the role can lead you to lose sight of the difference, and cause problems for you.

Lesson 11- Anchor yourself.

Distinguish yourself from your role. A healthy sense of self is rooted in character, not your elected title and/or position. Stay true to yourself.

> *Again, distinguishing yourself from your role is just as important with regard to praise as it is to criticism. When you begin to believe all of the good things people are saying about you, can you lose yourself in your role, distorting your personal sense of identity and self-image. Also people can gain control over you because of your desire to maintain their approval. Losing yourself in your role is a sign that you depend on the institution or community for meeting too many of your personal needs* (Kaur, 2002, p. 6).

One of the ways Ron anchored himself was by asking the community to call him by his name and not his title. Community members, out of respect, would call him "Mr. Mayor." With that mind, he would always kindly reply by saying to them, "Mayor is my title, Ron is my name."

Former California State Assemblymember Rich Gordon remembers when he realized that he had lost his first name about a year in the Legislature. Nobody ever called him Rich anymore. It was always "assemblyman" or "chairman" or "Mr. Gordon." And everybody wanted to do all kinds of things for him. He feels that having a spouse who is grounded can help keep you grounded and humble as well. Rich first ran for office in 1992, he was the first openly gay candidate for the San Mateo County Board of Supervisors. And when he was elected, he quickly found that his values and his identity were not popular among his peers.

Rich and his husband Denny recounted an occasion when he had to not only reveal himself as gay but stay true to himself. It was during a closed session and the discussion dealt with employee benefits for schoolteachers. Most of his colleagues in the room did not want to offer benefits to same-sex domestic partners of school employees.

As a gay man who strongly supported LGBTQ+ rights, he knew he would have to allow himself to be vulnerable among his peers. Rich saw his duty was to broaden the perspective of his colleagues and put a human face on the impact of this policy debate.

Rich shared, "It's not always easy, but as an elected official you must own who you are, know what you stand for, and be able to take a clear stand on issues, even if it's not the most popular one."

Ash Kalra, currently a California Assembly-member, said that too often representatives are focused only on getting re-elected. He advises candidates and officials to make their decisions based on their principles, not on the potential impact on reelection. Live by knowing what you stand for. If you act without principles, you are not doing your job.

Chappie Jones was always very clear with himself that he didn't want to be a part of "politics of personal destruction." He said his easy-going personality and his desire to be very respectful and kind to everyone was seen as a weakness by some in the political arena.

But he anchored himself in who he was at his core, his "why," and his passion for serving his community. He lived by the rule that he wouldn't say anything behind someone's back that he wouldn't say to them directly. Chappie's political philosophy was that you don't have to be disagreeable to disagree.

When Letitia Clark first ran for Tustin City Council as a young, Black woman in a predominantly white community, her motives were questioned. "For a woman of color, there's a common perception that you are running for some reason, like you're a mom who's angry about something in her neighborhood. But people generally don't ask that same question of men because they assume that men should run for office–that's the plan for men, not for women."

Letitia felt compelled to lead and she was tested during her first election when a prominent local elected official recommended that she shouldn't put her picture on her campaign mailers. Without her picture voters couldn't tell she was Black, and perhaps that would improve her chances to win. Letitia understood where this recommendation was coming from in this community. But she anchored herself in her desire to lead, her clear understanding of why she was running, and who she was. She didn't hide from her community, and she put her picture on all her mailers.

When she walked precincts, she quickly found common ground with voters by reminding them that she, like them, was also a "Tiller" first, referencing the Tustin High School mascot and a third-generation Tustin resident. She raised the most money ever for a city council campaign, and she won her first election by a strong margin.

By knowing and valuing yourself, distinct from the roles you play, you gain the freedom to take risks within those roles. Your self-worth is not so tightly tied to the reaction of other people as the content with your positions on issues. Moreover, you gain the freedom to take on a new role once the current one concludes or you hit a dead-end. No role is big enough to express all who you are. Each role you take on-parent, spouse, child; professional, friend, and neighbor, [elected official]- is a vehicle for expressing a different facet of yourself. Anchored in yourself, and recognizing and respecting your distinct roles, you are much less vulnerable to the pains of leadership (Kaur, 2002, p.14-15).

We hope that by anchoring yourself, it allows you to witness and learn throughout this experience, refining the core values that guide your decisions, regardless of whether they conform to public expectations or not. By anchoring yourself, we hope that you will be able to stay true to your "why."

Chapter 3 Lessons

Lesson 9: Once in office understand that you don't know everything.

Lesson 10: Manage your schedule. Manage your priorities. Manage your office.

Lesson 11: Anchor yourself.

CHAPTER 4

Pitfalls Of Public Service

"An enemy will stab you in the back, but a friend stabs you in your chest." -Former U.S. Representative and former Transportation Secretary Norman Y. Mineta

What did Norm Mineta mean by that quote? *We* believe he meant that in the intense world of politics, you have two types of people you will interact with: friends and allies.

Allies are with you if it is convenient for them and their agendas, and they may turn away from you when it is not convenient for them. *Friends* are with you no matter what, even if you disagree on policy, and they will be honest and forthright with you. But friends and allies are sometimes hard to distinguish. And there will be times when allies will become enemies, especially after they "stab you in the back."

Norm Mineta meant that only a false friend can do something wretched behind your back and not have the decency to do it to your face. Unfortunately, this is all too often the reality of politics.

Lesson 12 –Learn to differentiate between "allies" and "friends."

Though allies are essential for you to make progress toward your goals, they may be with you only when it is convenient. Friends are people who you can speak to and hear the truth, share your thoughts and emotions, and give you straight advice. You can disagree without worrying that your conversation will be used against you. You don't have to manage what and how much you say to friends. But with allies you need to mindfully manage the information and plans you share. Unfortunately, the nature of politics produces many more allies than friends. So, walk cautiously!

Allies are people who share many of your values, or at least your strategy, and operate across some organizational or factional boundary. Because they cross a boundary, they cannot always be loyal to you; they have other ties to honor. In fact, a key aspect of what makes allies extremely helpful is precisely that they do have other loyalties. That means they can help you understand competing stakes, conflicting views, and missing elements in your grasp of a situation. They can pull you by the collar to the balcony and say, "Pay attention to these other people over here. You're not learning anything from your enemies." Moreover, if persuasive, they can engage their people in the effort, strengthening your coalition.

Sometimes however, we make the mistake of treating an ally like a confidant. Confidants have few, if any, conflicting loyalties. They usually operate outside your organization's boundary, although occasionally someone very close in, whose interests are perfectly aligned with yours, can also play that role. You really need both allies and confidants.

Confidants can do something that allies can't do. They can provide you with a place where you can say everything that's in your heart, everything that's on your mind, without being predigested or well packaged. The emotions and the words can come out topsy-turvy, without order. Then once the whole mess is on the table, you can begin to pull the pieces back in and separate what is worthwhile from what is simply ventilation (Kaur, 2002, p. 15)

Differentiating between friends and allies can be a hard lesson to learn.

For Ron, it took him 24 years to learn this lesson, the hard way, and it came as a painful, public, personal, and expensive lesson. Towards the end of his second mayoral term, an ambitious deputy district attorney tried turning normal politics (a city council vote) into a criminal act. The council vote was related to avoiding a strike by the garbage collection workers and ensuring uninterrupted service. Except for just one council member, the city council voted to avoid the strike and approve a raise for the workers.

In the next election year, three sitting council members were running to succeed Ron as Mayor. They chose to use a 10-1 council vote to falsely say that Ron abused his position as mayor to get the raise for garbage workers and avoid a strike.

All but two council members turned on Ron, to his surprise and dismay. Some he had supported as candidates and mentored when they were new elected officials, and one had even once worked for him as a staff member. This same person, a candidate for mayor, tried to separate herself from him by saying "Ron was not her friend" in one of her campaign mailers. Yet, she had supported the same vision for the city and region. It was certainly a painful discovery that she really wasn't a friend, but rather an opportunistic ally.

It took many years for us to work through the pain of this experience that affected our whole family. Ron's mother and Guisselle's parents never forgave the loudest naysayers and never voted for any of them again.

Finally, six months after Ron termed out, Santa Clara County Superior Court Judge Herlihy dismissed the case in its entirety. Ron was vindicated, but it was at a high cost to fight for justice and his reputation for two years. It put our family and true friends through the trauma of emotional and financial hardship. It was an expensive lesson to learn, for we had to spend a half million dollars (provided by a line of credit and additional help from Guisselle's family) for Ron's legal defense.

Fortunately, this type of issue doesn't occur very often. But when it does, the collateral damage can reverberate for years across your personal and professional lives. Learn the lesson of distinguishing between allies and friends before it becomes public, painful, and expensive.

"You're a politician for a certain amount of time. Don't lose sight of your friends and family." -Madison Nguyen, former San Jose Vice Mayor, and Councilmember

Friends and refuge

Once you are elected you will find an abundance of new "fast friends" who want to come into your circle. Be careful of their motives and desires; some will only be with you while you are in office, and when you leave, they will move on to be "friends" with the next elected official. This doesn't mean you don't show up authentically with any of them, but it does underline the need to distinguish them from those in your true circle of friends.

Ash Kalra has made it a point to not let his political world also become his social world. He's careful to not mingle both worlds and keeps his private life private.

Rich Gordon reminded us that as an elected official the world feeds your ego. He's grateful to have a spouse and family to remind him that he was just another human being.

Spouses Rosanne Foust and Jim Hartnett, both (met and) served in elected office at the same time for the same city, shared that playing gin rummy, with each other, at least three times a week helped keep them grounded and relaxed, and allowed them to spend time together away from the distractions and demands of public office.

Susan and Steve Ellenberg told us that her campaign was an overwhelming priority in their lives, and that it took them two years to get back to some normality with their friends and their social life. Susan understands the importance of having her circle of friends, and she's making a conscious effort to stay in touch with them.

If you could make friends with elected colleagues, then you will be fortunate. It's not impossible, but inevitably other political loyalties and priorities may intervene with friendship. Be sure to maintain your circle of friends and family outside of politics that you can use as your sanctuary from the daily challenges, decisions and pressures that will come your way.

Disappointing supporters and friends

Lesson 13- Know when and how to say "no."

This was one of Ron's core principles ever since he disagreed about a public project a "supporter and friend" was involved in. He also learned that if you are going to say "no" to a friend, then say it as early as possible. Just like distinguishing between allies and friends, where a friend can disagree with you but will let you know, and why, because they care.

Nobody likes being turned down without explanation or apology, especially by someone close, and especially if it comes as a surprise. Friends and supporters deserve the respect to hear where you stand before you vote in public.

Ron recalls such an experience early in his public service career as a Sunnyvale City Councilmember. A developer was proposing a large project on a historically significant former fruit cannery site. The original cannery buildings weren't salvageable, but

Ron wanted to preserve its water tower as a salute to the orchard industry that predated Silicon Valley.

The water tower wasn't in the developer's plans, and Ron didn't want him to spend time and money trying to push the project through only to be turned down by the city council because of a new condition sprung by surprise. So, Ron explained his position and the likelihood that other council members also wanted to save the water tower.

The developer understood and was thankful for the early heads up. Four decades later the cannery water tower still stands as an iconic landmark commemorating a bygone era when Silicon Valley was better known as the Valley of Heart's Delight.

Negativity, an unfortunate by product of public service

"People take pride when you're knocked down or when you go through a difficult time. People resent success. You must embrace [the crap] and get over it. Keep your head up high and keep doing what you do." -Rosanne Foust, former Redwood City, Councilmember

Sadly, it's become commonplace for elected officials to be exposed to frequent hostility via social media or in the news media, and it isn't hidden from families and friends. This is a constant burden to elected officials and the people they're close to, and it can feel like hostile working conditions with no place to take your complaint.

But the unfortunate reality is that elected officials are not perceived in the same way as people in other, less public, occupations. Elected officials are fair game for criticism, and in our American democracy, it's always been this way. However, you can learn how to manage it.

Lesson 14. Come to terms with negativity and learn to manage it.

Rich Gordon's husband Denny quickly learned during one of Rich's first campaigns how much he was affected by reading the terrible comments from the media and public. To protect himself, he stopped reading the newspapers until Rich was elected.

But he now jokes that he follows the Irish philosophy of "don't get mad, get even." In one contentious race, one of Rich's opponents was named DeVille who was slinging a lot of mud. It so happened that the movie "101 Dalmatians," featuring the villain Cruella DeVille, was in theaters that year. Denny bought a "101 Dalmatians" necktie that Rich could wear to debates– it was Denny's quiet way of getting even. By the way, Rich won that election.

Carmen Stone said when her husband Larry was a Sunnyvale City Councilmember, some of his opponents even called her at home to tell her Larry was being an unfaithful husband with city employees. She knew it was false, stupid, and nasty, so she was able to ignore the calls.

San Jose City Councilmember Chappie Jones' wife, Kelli Jones, admitted it was difficult hearing people, especially those who were close, say untrue and negative things about your partner. It was something she wasn't prepared for as the spouse of an elected official. She decided early on to grant herself permission to handle such situations in her own way, even if it was different from Chappie's style. She just wasn't going to force herself to warmly greet someone who fabricated lies about her husband.

Setting boundaries and developing productive methods for handling negativity is critical to your own health and your partner's success. When do you confront it head on, and when do you let it slide? How will negativity affect your children, who are watching your responses? What is your comfort zone, and when do you have to get out of it? Thinking this through ahead of time will help when you're inevitably put in these situations.

During Raul Peralez's first San Jose City Council campaign, he had to help his mother Denise understand she couldn't take negative comments on social media personally. She saw the hateful comments on his posts and would immediately engage with the online trolls. That kind of response only adds fuel to the fire, and it risks making the damage worse, last longer, and spread further.

Raul had to ask his mother to stop responding, and she changed her tactics. Whenever she saw hateful comments on his posts she would still respond, but now she responded only by saying, "I love you, Son."

Rosanne Foust and Jim Hartnett remember the time when he and their good friend Pete were walking precincts on behalf of their wives who were both campaigning for the Redwood City Council. They had a run-in with a resident who wasn't so happy to meet them at the door and asked gruffly what they wanted. Pete answered they were campaigning for their wives.

The resident yelled back and said, "them sons of bitches!"

Pete took great offense and yelled back, "What did you say?" And suddenly a shouting match ensued. Anticipating something could go wrong with this heated debate, Jim pulled Pete from the porch, and they left without anybody getting hurt.

It's a warning, however, that emotions can run hot when someone verbally assaults your family, and it's all too easy to get sucked into the moment. You can laugh later, but it also could turn into a bad headline if you can't manage insults from ignorant people.

Letitia Clark said that negativity comes with the territory. Her formula for staying emotionally healthy included not reading anything online, such as social media and neighborhood apps, after council meetings or before she went to sleep. She used to dive into social media after the meetings and respond to negative comments. She had to learn not to do either, or instead she started to practice positive reaffirmation to remind herself to see people coming from the best possible intention, even if they disagreed. Hard to do, but important to try it.

Police sometimes had to escort Letitia from city hall to her car because of social media ugly threats to her and her family. But she continued to remind herself that trolls were not common in her community, and she trusted there is more good than bad. She's not naive, and she knows negativity and ugliness do exist. But she also knows you can't let that guide your ability to lead.

She also said "it's hard to hate up close," so she started coffee meetings with people who disagreed with her. She said that nine times out of ten they'd walk away with common interests and an open channel of communication and agree to disagree. Her trick for managing negativity was just to not "give it a lot of life."

Criticism of your public policy positions have become increasingly more personal, as former San Jose Mayor Sam Liccardo and his wife Jessica Garcia-Kohl experienced. During the "Black Lives Matter" civil rights rallies, some demonstrators vandalized their home with graffiti and a similar incident happened to Oakland Mayor Libby Schaaf. Mayors have always had their fair share of criticism but it's serious when your own home is attacked.

After the incident, Mayor Liccardo was gracious in his public comments and rose above anger. "Having someone graffiti my house is just part of the job. I understand that's the nature of leadership in difficult times" (Angst, 2020).

His quote reminded us of the paradox of public service. While you're facing incessant demands and criticism, you often must also manage other people's emotions without showing your own. When you are experiencing negativity on a regular basis, it can become a heavy load to hide your own feelings because of your role, mission, brand, and message.

Cindy Chavez admits that if she knew then what she knows now, she might have never run for office, but that it doesn't take away from the fact of how important the work we do is regardless of the people we serve.

Managing negativity can be exhausting, so we recommend that you find support for the psychological pressures of the job. Building boundaries, creating time for yourself, or finding a trusted and confidential counselor are ways to help. If you want to be an elected official who is fit, healthy, and able to make good policy decisions to achieve your goals, then provide yourself with support and respite.

Chapter 4 Summary of Lessons-

Lesson 12: Learn to differentiate between "allies and friends."

Lesson 13: Know when and how to say "no."

Lesson 14: Come to terms with negativity and learn to manage it.

CHAPTER 5

PREPARE FOR LIFE
AFTER PUBLIC OFFICE

Many people experience a rude awakening when they leave high positions of authority. Former CEOs and politicians alike find that their phone calls to important and busy people do not get through as easily, their emails are not answered as quickly, and their requests for favors and special treatment from "friends" no longer get quick results. Such is the harsh realization that the benefits they enjoyed in the past were at least as much a function of the role they played, the position they held, as they were a product of their character (Kaur, 2002, p.3).

Political terms come to an end. As we mentioned earlier, it's important to distinguish between your role as an elected official and your own self. If you become caught up in your role, if you believe that you are what your title is, then what adjustments will you have to make when you lose an election or leave office?

Lesson 15: There's life after the lime-light, but you need to be ready for it.

Many elected officials who leave office are forced to realize they are merely ordinary citizens again. It can be a rude awakening for some who have lost sight of who they really are. Politicians who lost or no longer serve in office are yesterday's news. Madison Nguyen is a former two-term San Jose City Councilmember and Vice Mayor remembers her moment of epiphany. She attended a community event after losing an election, and the event organizers didn't give her a title for her nametag. Her name was spelled correctly, but since she was no longer in office her title was "N/A."

Fortunately, she found the humor in it and shared it on social media:

Her social media post said, "Is this what happens after one loses an election?" This is a perfect illustration for our overall theme–distinguishing your public role from your own self will help you navigate both life in office, and life after with less recognition, fewer accolades, and limited access. Can you live with that?

Sometimes it's the spouse who enjoys the perks of office, the spotlight, and the access. We remember the spouse of a former city council member who told us how much he missed his wife being in office–he missed being invited to events, attending community activities, and getting attention as the spouse of an elected official.

Preparing for your life after leaving office applies to both those serving and their spouses, because public service is more than a job; it's a vocation. It's a gift, not a career.

Your purpose is to make an impact, not gratification from recognition and power. When you regard public service as a vocation, you can then distance yourself from the role and its trappings, and it becomes easier to gracefully leave when the time comes.

Your transition

Here are some ideas on how you can prepare for life after elected office.

1. Get your plans in place. At least one to two years before your term is over, think about your next chapter. Will you go back to your previous career? Do you have new professional opportunities? What income will you need to meet your financial needs?

2. Include your spouse in this conversation about the transition. How will it affect them? How will it affect your family?

3. Start researching how your elected experience could translate to your old or new career. What skills or experiences are transferable or valuable for a new path? Do you want to continue to serve your community? What would that look like for you and/or your family?

4. Talk to other former elected officials about their transitions, and about what they learned and what they might have done differently.

Ron served as a part-time elected official for many years, and his professional career was as an executive at the Hewlett Packard Company. After he served two terms as a County Supervisor, he resumed his career at Hewlett Packard. He then returned to politics and served eight years as San Jose Mayor. Out of office again, he decided to form his own marketing and sales consulting business. Eventually, he decided to go back to a different kind of public service, and since 2009 he has served as the President & CEO of a regional nonprofit organization focused on helping the Latino community.

After losing her bid for San Jose Mayor, Madison Nguyen became an executive for the local chamber of commerce, then as an executive for a media company. However, she said she missed public service, and is currently a candidate for the Santa Clara County Board of Supervisors.

Former San Jose Councilmember Raul Peralez also lost his race for Mayor, and he decided to return and serve as a San Jose police officer.

Jim Hartnett entered public life, first as a city Councilmember and Mayor for Redwood City, then as CEO of SamTrans, a regional transportation agency. His wife Rosanne Foust, former Redwood City Councilmember, currently serves as President and CEO of the San Mateo County Economic Development Association.

Rich Gordon served two decades in public service, from a school board trustee to San Mateo County Supervisor to California State Assembly-member. He is now President and CEO for the California Forestry Association.

Letitia Clark continues to serve on the Tustin City Council and has two more years in her term. She is currently weighing her options for what to do next. She said that once you're on the political "hamster wheel," you feel like you can't stop; people will pressure you to continue to serve in other capacities. She has been advised and enticed to run for another local office, or congress, or the state legislature, but she knows she first must understand what those other roles look like and require as a candidate and as an office holder.

She's aware that this courting is flattering, so she's anchoring herself by reminding herself to listen to what is true to her before jumping in again. She's reflecting on what she has been able to accomplish in her two full terms in office and is considering focusing now on her full-time job and more time with her kids before they graduate from high school.

These are not easy decisions, but her situation again reminds us that your "why" always needs to be clear regardless of your position and your plans.

As you consider your next steps, take some time for reflection, speak to your family, and do your homework. Don't be flattered in the courting, reassess your why, and think about what's best for you and your family. Don't get anxious when people tell you must run now before you lose your name recognition, your network of support, and your momentum. Don't get FOMO, fear of missing out. Remember, those who are pushing you to run for another seat might not be there for you if you do decide to go for it.

If you feel you've accomplished what you set out to do and have done a good job, and you're not feeling the call to run for office at this moment, then you can always run later. If you have a good track record, you will be remembered when the time does come. But if you truly feel the call, and your "why" is clear and strong, then go for it.

Chapter 5 Summary of Lessons-

Lesson 1   There's life after the limelight, but you need to be ready for it.

Epilogue: After The Lessons...

"Service is love in action." Archbishop of Canterbury Justin Welby

There will be many times when serving will be challenging and difficult but there will also be good times that you'll remember more–the times you got the votes; the important groundbreakings and ribbon cuttings; moving the needle for greater opportunity, justice, and quality of life for the people you serve.

When surveyed, 88% of our interviewees said, knowing what they know now, they would still run for elected office again. They cite the desire to serve and the opportunity to shape public policy for the common good as the main driver to want to serve again. Our interviewees say their proudest accomplishments revolve around the following themes: bringing the community together, social justice, economic development, environmental issues, affordable housing, and building infrastructure.

Cindy Chavez said it well, "running for office is almost counterintuitive. You don't know what you don't know before you run." People have come to her hesitant about the negativity they'll experience during the campaign. But Cindy feels these would-be candidates are the people we need in public service, despite, or maybe because of the challenges they will face.

We need people who are empathetic, who have a vision and good ideas, and who have a strong desire to make their communities a better place to live for all their residents. Cindy is glad now that she didn't know what she didn't know before running for office, and that she was able to serve successfully.

However, we believe that in this era of social media, polarized politics, and instant communication, the stakes are much higher now for candidates and their families. Being equipped with knowledge of what to expect will help you and your family be better prepared, more resilient, and more likely to be successful.

Yes, there are challenges, but there's also inspiration. Yes, you can serve and make your community better! And you're not alone.

Just as the people we have interviewed for this book have inspired others to serve, your journey can also provide inspiration and support for someone else. Share your knowledge, share your stories and your struggles, and share your successes so that you may inspire someone else to run and continue the hard work of public service.

Our hope is that the lessons we have shared will help inform you to make the best decision for you and your family. And if you are currently in elected office, or choose to serve in elected office, our hope is that these lessons can lay the foundation for you to be able to thrive and succeed in the political fishbowl.

What do they wish they knew then that they know now?

Steve and Lisa Guerrero- *They both wish Steve had done his homework before he launched his (unsuccessful) campaign. They both agree that Steve's decision should have been made with Lisa. Steve had no idea what a campaign required, let alone what it meant to be on the school board.*

Raul Peralez and Victoria Ramirez- *They both wish they knew what this political lifestyle would involve. Raul said that it was confusing trying to learn along the way as he asked different people for their perspectives, advice and their stories. Raul said, "The problem with doing that on your own is that you're hearing 100 different perspectives and trying to keep track of it all while figuring out the campaign." Raul also wishes someone would have told him that every year in office would be different and that it would require different things from you and your family.*

Steve and Susan Ellenberg- *They wish they knew that once you make the decision to run for office, the negativity would start to show up in the newspapers and social media. They would have liked to have known that they needed to prepare not only themselves but also their families, including their parents, siblings, etc.*

Chappie and Kelli Jones- *Chappie wishes he had known how to better manage his case of impostor syndrome, where he felt he wasn't ready and prepared for the role. Additionally, he wishes he had known how to better manage his calendar and how important it was to prioritize a regular day off for rest. Kelli wishes she knew how to better manage the negativity and to learn how to not hold grudges against people who say negative things about your spouse during the campaign. It will always feel personal, but you must find a way to separate yourself from the situation.*

Rich Gordon and Dennis McShane- *They would have liked to have known how important it was to always keep the lines of communication open in their relationship. Rich's dad used to say, "Never let the sun go down on your anger." Rich says, "in other words, if you're having an argument with your spouse, you settle up before you go to bed. It's good advice."*

Larry and Carmen Stone- *Larry wished he knew as a "newbie" running for office that he was going to live three lives: his family life, his professional life, and his political life. He said that a newbie needs to understand that you are going to spend a lot of time away from home learning everything you need to know about your new role in politics.*

Ash Kalra- *He wishes he knew two things "that once you're in, you're in. You start off running and it never stops. In fact, the pace of the role only gets faster. You must learn how to manage your time to keep up." And second, he didn't know how important it would be for him to keep parts of his private life, such as relationships, out of social media, so that he could still have some personal time, and space in his personal life.*

Cindy Chavez and Mike Potter- *Cindy would have liked to have known "how ugly and snarky journalists and reporters can be in the media. It's the one thing you can't control but it's better to be prepared on how to handle it."*

Mike's advice "is to never run the campaign out of your house. The one place of peace must be your home and running a campaign at home completely takes that away."

Dave and Pattie Cortese- *At the beginning of his political career, Dave began as a school board member while finishing law school at night, running his business, studying, and passing the state bar exam, and raising his small children. With all of this going on, he decided to also run for state assembly. Now he wishes that "he would have slowed down long enough to have appropriate conversations with his loved ones." He wants other candidates to know that there isn't a rush to do all those things at one time at the expense of your family's needs and your own mental and emotional well-being.*

Doug and Nadine Horner- *Doug wants to share with young, elected officials "that they don't need to be as nice and conciliatory to the rest of their colleagues. But to drive harder for the things that they believe in." He believes he waited too long to get to that place where he was able to stand and lead on the issues, he believed in. A mentor taught him "that it doesn't matter what you say, or how eloquent your speeches are, just fine-tuning works. It's all about finding the right votes."*

Madison Nguyen and Terry Tran- *Madison wishes that before she decided to run for office, she would have taken more time to meet with more current and former elected officials to learn about their experiences. She also wishes she would have taken more time to get to know her local community and become better versed in political nuances and dynamics. She recommends that before you make your decision to run, you spend at least one year doing your homework, finding mentors, and learning more about the role and the community you want to serve.*

Rosanne Foust and Jim Hartnett- *Rosanne recommends that if your family is a priority, then consider elected roles that will fit with your family's schedule. Her children were always her priority, so she chose elected roles that gave her the flexibility to be with her children as much as possible.*

And she said, don't take things personally. It'll save you a lot of energy and time.

Jim's advice is to have discussions with your family before deciding to run for office. He feels that's something he did not do when he first got into politics, which negatively affected his first marriage. His former spouse felt like he was abandoning his family and focusing on the wrong things in life. Jim admits he did not know what to expect when he first decided to run and underestimated the time commitment. He saw how his family was affected by that decision, and thus he strongly recommends bringing your family into your discussion and decision to run for office.

Letitia Clark- Letitia would have liked to have understood the idea of "fast friends" and learn to be more discerning. Though "fast friends" are not malicious in their intent, they want access and favors. Her family has experienced this with "fast friends" who have invited her husband to special events pretending to be his friend or have scheduled playdates with her kids just so that the parents could have access to Letitia. Recognize who are "fast friends," and keep your real friends closer.

What about the authors of this book? What do we wish we knew then that we know now?

Guisselle Nuñez- *I would have liked to have under-stood the difference between allies and friends. Knowing that this was a natural byproduct of political life, it would have made it easier to forgive (not necessarily forget), which would have brought her more inner peace throughout the many chal-lenges that came while Ron served in office.*

Ron Gonzales- *I would have liked to have known the difference between allies and friends. I took it for granted that 24 years of public elected service record would valorize my integrity, and thus "friends" would never question my integrity. But in fact, I didn't know that those friends could easily become "allies" who were willing to attack my integrity, and sacrifice my public record of accomplishments, for their political gain.*

Angst, M. (2020, August 31). *Vandalism of San Jose mayor's homes takes protests to a new level.* The Mercury News. https://www.mercurynews.com/2020/08/31/vandalism-of-mayors-homes-takes-protests-to-a-new-level/

CBS 17. (2021, March 10). *Video: CBS newsman Roger Mudd interviews Teddy Kennedy.* YouTube. https://www.youtube.com/watch?v=ZX-ORTribU2Q

Flinders, M., Weinberg, A., Weinberg, J., Geddes, M., & Kwiatkowski, R. (2018). Governing under pressure? The mental wellbeing of politicians. *Parliamentary Affairs.* https://doi.org/10.1093/pa/gsy046

Gaughan, L. (2022, March 6). *Why 'The candidate' is still a cautionary tale fifty years later.* Collider. https://collider.com/the-candidate-cautionary-tale-explained/

Geha, J. (2023, January 20). *Allegations surface against San Jose council hopefuls.* San José Spotlight. https://sanjosespotlight.com/allegations-surface-against-san-jose-city-council-hopefuls/

Imperial War Museums. (2018). *Darkest Hour - Kristin Scott Thomas and Clementine Churchill.* YouTube. https://www.youtube.com/ watch?v=q2Hhk5GLfSM&t=1s

Kaur. (2002). Chapter 9. In *Leadership on the line: Staying alive through the dangers of leading* (pp. 3-15). Harvard Business School Publishing Corporation.

Moss, J. (2022, December 29). *An entrance interview with Matt Mahan, San Jose's 66th mayor.* Silicon Valley Business Journal. https://www.biz-journals.com/sanjose/news/2022/12/30/ matt-mahan-entrance-interview.html

Pascoe, B. (2009, November 5). *The candidate what do we do now.* YouTube. https://www.youtube. com/watch?v=myEpap3TxVs

Weinberg, A. (2021, April 16). *A politician's mental health is as crucial as a pilot's. Why don't we tend to it.* The Washington Post. https://www.wash-ingtonpost.com/outlook/2021/04/16/ politicians-mental-health-dan-kildee/

Ron Gonzales

Ron Gonzales' personal philosophy is to help improve the quality of life for others. This philosophy has guided his 45-plus years of technology, public policy, and non-profit professional experience. Currently, Ron serves as President and CEO of the Hispanic Foundation of Silicon Valley. He served as Mayor of San José, the Capital of Silicon Valley and the nation's 10th-largest city from 1999-2006. He also served for eight years (1989-1996) on the Santa Clara County Board of Supervisors and was a two-time mayor and member of the Sunnyvale, CA, City Council (1979-87).

Guisselle Nuñez

Guisselle is focused on helping organizations and individuals achieve success through enduring marketing and personal branding strategies. Currently, she's Associate Vice President, Strategic Marketing Communications for San Francisco State University and serves as the chief marketing officer for the university. She's an award-winning marketing communications leader, speaker, and author of the book "Take Charge of your Brand." A former political spouse for twenty years, she continues to coach many political spouses, candidates, and elected officials on how to manage their personal brands and navigate life while serving in public office.